CRACKING THE GLOBAL MARKET

CRACKING THE GLOBAL MARKET

How to Do Business Around the Corner and Around the World

Jack Nadel

amacom

American Management Association

This book is available at a special
discount when ordered in bulk quantities.
For information, contact Special Sales Department,
AMACOM, a division of American Management Association,
135 West 50th Street, New York, NY 10020.

Library of Congress Cataloging-in-Publication Data

Nadel, Jack.
    Cracking the global market.

    Includes index.
    1. Commerce. 2. Export sales. 3. United States—
Commerce. 4. Export sales—United States. 5. Competition,
International. I. Title.
HF1008.N33 1987   658.8'48   87-47703
ISBN 0-8144-5911-0

Printing number

10 9 8 7 6 5 4 3 2 1

To
ELLY,
with love,
who shared it all and shares it all . . .

Acknowledgments

I would like to give special thanks to Beverly Cohn, who was my executive secretary when I started to write this book in 1983. She is now vice president of our newly formed division, MMS Trading. Beverly kept insisting that what I did on a daily basis should be passed on. She not only persuaded me to write the book, but she transcribed the tapes and was even able to decipher my longhand scribbling. When the first very rough draft was completed, Beverly did the seemingly impossible. She persuaded a recognized literary agent to read it and take me on as a client.

Sherry Robb, who I fondly call the Bette Midler of the literary set, felt that the book had great potential, but needed a lot of work. She took great pains to help me write an outline, which she submitted along with the complete manuscript. I have enormous appreciation for the great amount of time that she spent on a mature businessman who had never written anything for publication. She performed a minor miracle when she sold my still disorganized book to a strong publisher.

I am very grateful to Ron Mallis, Director of Corporate Product Development of AMACOM, who bought the book and became my editor. Ron had read every word of my ramblings and had enough faith to make the deal. I am very grateful for all the time he took and the professional suggestions that he made. His patience and perception helped to sharpen the book.

Sherry then introduced me to Trevor Meldal-Johnsen, who undertook the task of organizing my material into cohesive order. Trevor and I spent many hours together reworking the manuscript. We clarified points and added material in response to his probing questions. My words emerged clearer and stronger thanks to Trevor's fine professional hand and his comprehension.

Most importantly there is my wife, Elly, who read it all as it was written; criticizing, commenting, and questioning all the way. Her constant support was essential, as many commitments were set aside in favor of spending time on the book. It all became worthwhile when she read the last words of the final paragraph. Her eyes misted and she said: "Great." This was my first and most important review.

Contents

Introduction

Forty years bring vast changes to a man's life—and to his world. When World War II ended and I left the U.S. Air Force to take my first sales job, Japan and Germany were in rubble, and a victorious America was enjoying the spoils. During the next decade, America dominated the world with its culture, its science, its economy, and its trade.

Times have changed. That "Happy Days" world has come and gone, and a new war is being fought in the arena of international trade. A day doesn't go by without media comment on America's lopsided trade balance and the crucial need to increase exports. The tremendous shifts that have occurred in the economic balance of power have long since obscured the lines between enemies and allies, and all developed nations have become fierce competitors in today's marketplace. American business once felt that the world was its ballpark, and that no one played without its permission. Now it is pitching a game it no longer controls and sometimes barely recognizes.

Many of us react to this trade crisis by crying for protectionist legislation, a move that would be both impractical and undesirable. Inflation is but one of many bad side effects of a blind "Buy America" policy. Experience also has shown that protectionism here begets protectionism abroad. It is a luxury we can't afford.

The ostrich impulse—ignore your problems and they'll go away—is another disastrous reaction. Detroit's mighty automotive empire shook and nearly crumbled when faced with the popularity of high-quality, inexpensive, fuel-efficient competitors from Japan and the more elegant European imports. When Detroit finally responded to this market need, it was almost too late.

I believe that, in spite of our problems today, America not only can compete, but can dominate world markets. I do not think this a matter of choice or simply of something that's nice to do. It has become a question of survival.

To assume a leadership position, we must be willing to better understand the international marketplace. More than 75 percent of the world market lies beyond our borders, and we ignore this fact only at our peril. Ready or not, the world is competing with us in our own neighborhood.

Many opportunities lie in the "triad countries"—the United States and Canada, the industrial countries of Europe, and the expanding trade centers of Asia. Not only is this a logical and immensely profitable arena for American business, but it is an exciting adventure as well.

Over the past 40 years I have built a $100 million international company that is involved, on a daily basis, with both import and export. The Measured Marketing Services companies began with a 12-square-foot office, two used desks, a portable typewriter, and a $10,000 investment. Today, there are over 700 employees and 22 offices and factories throughout the United States, Europe, and the Orient. In spite of the economic upheavals of recent decades, my business has grown and continues to grow. This is fact, not self-congratulation. Constant adjustment to the realities of a shifting marketplace has kept me among the players. I didn't discover any magic formula 40 years ago, but I did adopt an attitude of flexible opportunism. Textbook formulas just don't work in the world of international trade, and the market quickly proves that to disbelievers. Experience has been my best teacher, and still continues to be.

When I speak to college students or young entrepreneurs, a common complaint is: "So you managed to build a $100 million business. But you started forty years ago when America was powerful and international opportunities were unlimited. How can we do that today?" My answer is that opportunities for both entrepreneurs and established American businesses are even greater today.

Amazing advances in communications and transportation have shrunk both time and space, making the world a smaller and much easier place in which to do business. Forty years ago the entrepreneur with a bright new idea found it virtually impossible to raise capital. Today, the market is filled with money-laden individuals and companies who actively seek worthy ideas in which to invest. The businessman willing to look beyond his traditional borders and embrace this vast marketplace called the world has virtually unlimited opportunities within his grasp. All that restrains him is his imagination and his courage.

The challenges and opportunities have never been greater in world trade. Some of us tend to make obstacles of challenges and see only unwelcome competition in a field rife with opportunity. But those of us who can perceive and estimate accurately the opportunities available are the ones who will achieve American dominance in the international marketplace.

In writing this book I hope to share with you the insights gained from four decades of experience in domestic and international business. There are, however, many ways to skin a cat, and my way is not necessarily the best. I am not speaking from the mount of absolute or infallible wisdom. I could no more have foreseen today's marketplace when I entered the business world after World War II, than I can now tell you what to export in the year 2026. I can show you some of the ground rules and what has worked for me over the years, in the hope that they will stimulate you and be of value.

I have learned that generally the business world makes every function far too complicated. International trade is no exception. Many American businesses stay away from this lucrative and rewarding field because fear and ignorance dominate their thoughts of what is involved. Furthermore, our nation's vast size has made trading within our own borders extremely profitable, and many have never been forced to look abroad to increase their market share. That time has come. We have no choice now but to compete.

My desire in this book is to demystify the process and show, not only that American business must adapt to changing world conditions, but that it is a relatively easy thing to do. The international entrepreneur is as old as civilized man; there have always been traders among us. What's new are today's abundant opportunities and the urgency for American business to understand them. Like it or not, this is one world. By recognizing this fact and taking advantage of it, our nation can once again attain the leadership position it seems to have abdicated. Those individuals and businesses willing to enter this bountiful international arena will prosper like never before.

I
Breaking the Ice

At its roots, all business is concerned with problem-solving. If you're a manufacturer, your problem is finding markets for your product. If you're an importer, your problem is finding goods that fill domestic market needs. Either way, the basic premise of "find a need and fill it" will lead you where you want to be.

Needs vary around the world; that is the challenge and the benefit of international trade. It may be easier to supply a need in your immediate area than one 10,000 miles away, but it may not be as profitable. If you draw from the same domestic sources as all competing suppliers, where is your advantage in the market? A manufacturer may prefer the comfort of dealing with people who speak the same language and where commerce is governed by the same laws, but if domestic sales are slow, all the comfort in the world won't move the inventory.

The global market place addresses all these common problems and contains the seeds of their solutions. It presents a tremendous range of needs and wide-ranging opportunities for imaginative entrepreneurs.

My beginnings in the field of international trade were humble. I started with little more than a drive to succeed. My older brother, Saul, was first to break the ice. He came to California in 1946 and, with the few dollars he borrowed from me and friends, he established an export-import business. I joined him to form a staff of two. We were entrepreneurs, even though the word wasn't used much in those days.

The world was reeling from the effects of a terrible war. Massive product shortages of all kinds created opportunities for anyone who could supply them—which is what we intended to do. We had no money, no experience, and only a little knowledge, but we knew enough to ask the question, "What product can we pursue that will give us a solitary advantage in the marketplace?"

We knew also that the U.S. military was selling cheaply an enormous amount of surplus war material, including olive drab woolen. We had to find a need for it, and although people all over the world wanted goods, few had the U.S. dollars to pay for it.

Our research turned up a need in China, and we heard also that the Chinese traders had the money. The only problem was that olive drab was not in demand there. The Chinese wanted blue material.

The first step was to go to the Chinese consulate and the foreign trade department of the Los Angeles Chamber of Commerce to get lists of Chinese importers who dealt in piece goods. Then we had to decide how to approach them.

Since we were in Los Angeles and expected to export to the Pacific area, we named our company Trans Pacific Traders. Next, we invested our few remaining dollars in some high quality stationery—far more impressive than our tiny office warranted. We reasoned that prospective customers would probably never see our office, but the stationery would serve as tangible evidence of some means.

We composed a short hard-sell letter. We introduced ourselves as an established (in fact, it had been only three weeks) export company with a large inventory of navy blue serge. We enclosed a swatch of the material and offered up to 100,000 yards at $3 per yard. We urged a quick response, since this bargain in scarce merchandise was subject to prior sale. Then we specified terms of payment by confirmed irrevocable letter of credit.

Twenty letters went out, each carefully typed and per-
sonalized to the names on our list. Rather than put them in
our corner mailbox, we took them to the post office to gain
an extra day. Both time and money were running out for our
grand experiment, but with the crazy optimism of youth, we
felt in our bones that this long shot would pay off.

While doing this, we made an arrangement with a surplus
dealer for him to buy, finance, and dye the material blue. We
would, we told him, sell it on a letter of credit and split the
profit. Our investment was, thus, very small.

For those unfamiliar with the concept, a letter of credit
is a guarantee by a bank to pay a specified amount when the
terms of a deal are met. If a merchant opens a letter of credit
in my favor, the bank pays me the particular amount when
I provide evidence that the goods have been shipped.

Though we didn't have much money invested in the venture, the wait was nerve-racking. To a large extent, our future
as independent businessmen was at stake.

A week passed, and there was no word. Ten days, and
still nothing. The strain began to wear on me. I wondered
where my next dollar would come from if our plan didn't
work. And I spent a few sleepless nights wondering if I would
be better off looking for a job.

Two weeks after sending the offering, we were both immensely relieved and delighted when we received the first cable
from an importing company in Shanghai. It was short, but
. . . oh, so sweet:

OUR LETTER OPENING L/C 5,000 YARDS NAVY
SERGE FOLLOWS. PLEASE ADVISE EARLIEST DE-
LIVERY

Our total cost for material and dyeing was $1.80 per yard.
We sold the 5,000 yards at $3 a yard, which gave us a net
profit of $6,000. It was a lot of money in those days, and
Trans Pacific Traders suddenly became a viable business.

We were performing the function of a trading company.
We found the demand and satisfied it. The need happened to

be 6,000 miles away, by people we would never meet, whose language we would never speak—and financed with money we did not have. But there was no risk once the deal was made. It was the first of many such transactions.

Our biggest deal demanded much more ingenuity. We discovered a need in China and India for caustic soda and soda ash, the chemicals used in the manufacture of soap and soap products. Utilizing similar research sources, such as the consulate and the chamber of commerce, and following up with letters, we located an Indian trader who wanted 2,000 tons of caustic soda. He was willing to pay $.12 a pound.

There was one major hitch. We didn't have the caustic soda. It was a strange situation. Although caustic soda was unavailable, there actually was no shortage. It was under federal price control and was sold by the mills for 4¢ a pound. But you couldn't buy it because, in 1947, it was impossible to get the 55-gallon steel drums to hold the chemical. At the time, nothing but steel could contain the soda, since it would eat through other materials.

We knew by now that we could sell caustic soda for 12¢ to 20¢ per pound. It was a great incentive to become inventive.

Saul and I made dozens of calls to Pittsburgh to find steel. Then Saul called on Southern Alkali, a company in Texas that was the largest producer of caustic soda in the U.S. He made a proposal. "If we can supply you with steel at the mill price," he asked, "will you be willing to supply us with caustic soda at the mill price?"

Of course they said yes. We had offered a solution to their only problem—getting steel for the drums. They were willing to do so if we provided twice as much steel as was needed for our order.

We contracted at a very high price with a small steel-rolling mill in Pittsburgh to provide the steel according to Southern Alkali's specifications. We overpaid for the steel and sold it to Southern Alkali at below our cost, losing money on every pound of steel. On the other hand, we were underpaying for the caustic soda. We factored the steel overpayment into the price at which we would sell the caustic soda and estimated that we would still make a handsome profit.

My job was to finance the deal—without money. We did it through back-to-back letters of credit. Our customer in India opened a letter of credit to us for 2,000 tons at 12¢ a pound, and we opened a letter of credit to Southern Alkali for the caustic soda at 4¢ a pound. We also opened a letter of credit to the steel company to cover the high price of the steel.

Because we were new to international trading, we had to convince the bankers we knew what we were doing. It was a giant juggling act requiring exquisite timing, great salesmanship, and a lot of nerve. When the letters of credit came due, our timing was off. I talked to the head of the bank's Foreign Trade Division, to persuade him to wait 24 hours until one end cleared so the other end could be paid.

It all worked. I had many moments of uncertainty, but not about the final result. Part of being an entrepreneur is knowing that the deal will work, in spite of evidence to the contrary. We sold 2,000 tons of caustic soda to India for $480,000 and made a net profit of $180,000. Not bad for novice international traders.

I learned a tremendous amount from Saul about making and selling deals. He was a flamboyant man and a brilliant trader who could put two ends of a deal together better and faster than anyone else I knew. More important, perhaps, by observing his mistakes, I also learned how *not* to operate a competitive business. Saul was a deal maker, not a business operator—two very different activities. His strengths did not include successfully operating a competitive business and overseeing a staff. He was a poor administrator, and he tended to surround himself with people who always agreed with him. Though it is comfortable, even encouraging, to have people around who say yes to everything you propose, it is not healthy. You don't attract the best people, and your mistakes go unchallenged. We had many stormy disagreements. Inevitably, we went our separate ways.

It remained a love-hate relationship right to the end. When Saul suffered from a bleeding ulcer and was forced to check into a hospital, I told him I would pick up the tab. I visited him and saw that, in typical grandiose style, he had taken a large private suite. It was predictable, but I still fought it. "Listen, Saul," I said. "I told you I'd pick up the tab, but I didn't say I'd pay for the Waldorf-Astoria. How come you took a suite?"

"I figured I'm not going to make it, so I thought I'd go out in style," he said.

For once I couldn't argue. Saul made it that time, but a few years later he died. It was a great loss for me.

Find a Need and Fill It

Whether importing, exporting, or selling on your neighborhood corner, the old saw of "find a need and fill it" applies. It applied when traders trudged across deserts and mountains with camels and donkeys, and it applies today in the age of jet travel and high-speed communications. But, like many truisms, it is sometimes easier said than done. How do you discover what and where the need is? And how do you overcome the barriers in filling it? In particular, for international trade where barriers of distance and language exist, how do you carve a niche for yourself?

It can be done. I have been successful by using the true meaning of that old saw; that is, not just trying to fill the *apparent* or *obvious* need, but looking more deeply to find the *real* need.

Every business deal involves a certain amount of flack: problems, opinions, and other things that tend to obscure the basic need. It reminds me of when I was flying a B-29 bomber over Japan during World War II. The enemy gunners would spot us on radar and fire at us. To distract the enemy guns, we created false targets by dropping silver foil that showed up on their radar screens. It's the same in business. There are a lot of false targets to distract you. You have to determine what is the silver foil and which is the real airplane.

Finding a need and filling it is not an abstract concept or an academic exercise, but a way of thinking that involves creativity and incentive. Perhaps some of my experiences will ignite your own creative abilities. For example, in October of 1949, after parting ways with my brother, I was hunting for a job. I was 26 years old and wide open to a new opportunity. I found the specialty advertising business, a business I have been in ever since.

Specialty advertising involves the sale of merchandise with some intrinsic value, which can be used for advertising purposes as well as business gifts. Generally, the products are various novelties that carry a company's imprint, and the company gives them as gifts to customers or prospects. A good example is a calendar, which the advertiser gives to his customers, getting his message exposed for the entire year.

I answered an advertisement for a specialty advertising salesman that appeared in the *Los Angeles Times*. I fulfilled all the qualifications: I could say three words in a row and my body was warm.

At that time, very few people knew or understood the specialty business. Seabury & Company was then the largest independent specialty advertising company in Los Angeles, but actually it was small. The leader in the field was Brown & Bigelow, out of St. Paul, Minnesota, with some 700 salespeople around the country.

Seabury's policy was simple. Send out anyone who could carry a line of samples, in the hope that he would find someone to sell to before becoming discouraged and moving on. There were no territories; salesmen could go where they wished. Equipped with my sales kit of lines of wooden yardsticks, emery boards, sewing kits, painter's caps, and nude calendars, I set off with a sense of adventure and not much practical knowledge.

During the first week I sold nothing, although I did become emotionally involved with the nude calendars. I didn't know whom to call on, and I didn't know the value of what I had. Nor was the company much help; sales training was a luxury in their minds. I didn't make a sale until the second week, and then I made the princely commission of $8.75 on a $35 sale of emery boards.

But I began to learn. Most of the salesmen thought they were selling products. But as I made call after fruitless call, I realized that this was in essence an advertising medium, and that I was not selling products but *ideas that manifested themselves in the form of products*. The idea was to promote the name, the product, or the image. Our product was the vehicle that carried their idea, pinpointed to the people who could influence a sale. My customer could give the specialties I sold him to people he was already selling to as well as to prospects. As these realizations grew, so did the knowledge that this was potentially a very profitable business.

I began to prove it. Using the idea concept and calling on people who had money to spend and a product or service to sell, I sold a $10,000 order in my second month. (In this business, a $500 order was a rarity.) Shortly after that, I sold a $16,000 order. In Seabury's history, no one had ever taken a $16,000 order.

One of the basics of entrepreneurship is to not follow the beaten path, but to start your own path. In January 1950, everyone knew it was impossible to sell because Christmas was over. In doing some client prospecting, however, I discovered an opportunity. Occidental Insurance had done calendar-card promotions in the past, and the cards were made of lightweight cardboard, which meant that after several month's use, they would fray and curl around the edges. Occidental's customers would use their cards only for a few months, diminishing the life of the company's promotional dollar.

I decided that plastic would have more permanence and could enable Occidental to keep its advertising message alive for a full year. I came up with a new layout using a glossy plastic. Besides changing the material and design, I added a bonus: I would reverse-print the holidays so they could be highlighted "at no extra charge to the customer for the additional color." Occidental was impressed enough to place a $6,000 order. The card was no earth-shaking innovation, but by being creative with materials and products that already existed, I found a way to make a unique and exciting product tailored to the needs of my client.

If the world is your marketplace and your source of supply, it is also the match to spark your creativity. About a month after I closed the Occidental deal, I was driving down Beverly Boulevard in Los Angeles and saw a billboard for East Side Beer. The caption read: "Winner of the Pan-American Exposition Award—1927." A large gold medallion shone in the lower right-hand corner of the billboard.

This was 1950, and the award was given in 1927. Obviously, the company was still proud of it, but I thought they could get a lot more from it than what a billboard could offer.

I drove directly to East Side Beer and asked for the sales manager. "I've got a terrific idea," I told him enthusiastically. "You know the billboards you have all over town. How would you like me to reproduce your 1927 gold medal and distribute it through every liquor store in the city? People would receive it with their change."

He agreed that it was a terrific idea and placed an initial order for 250,000 gold-coin reproductions at 6¢ each. Shortly, he repeated the 250,000 order and then placed an order for 500,000 units. People were eating the coins up.

I knew this was an interesting idea, but it wasn't *that* interesting. I couldn't figure out why the coins were so popular. I wasn't complaining; the order totaled $30,000. But why on earth did people keep coming back for more coins?

There are times when luck plays a part. It took me a while to discover it, but there was a reason: The coin fit the dollar slot machines in Las Vegas. People were playing the casino machines with East Side Gold Medal Award Winner—1927 coins!

Discovering a need and filling it involves associated skills: creativity, marketing, hard work, the ability to anticipate a client's problems and solve them, and, sometimes, a flair for show business—what some salespeople call "romance."

Early in my career I got into the habit of doing my customer prospecting by reading advertisements in newspapers and magazines. A well-done advertisement telegraphs a client's biggest selling point. By knowing what a client wanted to say, I could create an idea to help him say it. Years later I transferred this simple technique to international marketing, but in those formative times I was refining it.

I went to the Los Angeles County Fair in Pomona to get leads, and I asked for a copy of the exhibitor registration sheet. On it I recognized a company called Western Holly. I had seen their advertisements; they manufactured an 18-inch range, the largest capacity of any mass-produced oven on the market.

I don't know how the idea hit me. Maybe it was because I was selling yardsticks to builders at the time. But the ads said the ovens were 18 inches wide—half a yard. I saw the potential for a unique specialty item. If I could create a new product by cutting the yardstick in half, it would explain graphically how large the oven was; the yardstick would have plenty of room for advertising copy, it would be relatively inexpensive, and, most important, it could be a handy product to have around the home. Even if the potential buyer was not in the market for a range at the time, the ruler would be a constant reminder of the wonderful things he or she could do with additional oven capacity when ready to purchase one.

That night I rehearsed my pitch, and the next day I went to Western Holly's executive offices to see the director of marketing. "Are you going to the exhibit at the County Fair?" I asked, after we had chatted for a moment. When he said yes, as I knew he would, I asked what kind of literature they were going to distribute.

"We're in the process of preparing a number of brochures and fliers," he said.

"Tell me," I asked, "do you think they do much good?"

"Well," he said with a sheepish smile, "to tell you the truth, I think all they do is mess up the fairgrounds."

Knowingly or not, he had just agreed that he needed a better product. "Listen, I've got an idea for you," I said.

"What's that?" he asked.

I didn't answer at first. Instead, I took a yardstick from my bag and held it up. Then, suddenly, I brought it down fast and broke it over my knee.

"What the hell are you doing?" he asked, puzzled at my dramatics.

I handed him half the yardstick and said, "This is half-a-yard—18 inches—the exact size of your oven."

He took it and read what I had dummied on that half the night before:

Check This With Your Present Oven—Western Holly—
2+ Inches Larger.

"Your potential customers can actually use it to measure the capacity of their old ovens against yours," I explained. "Instead of giving out literature that people will throw away, why not give them a gift that they can carry with them and keep for a long time, reminding them of the Western Holly range?" He was thrilled, and responded by giving me an order for 100,000 18-inch rulers.

Part of any successful deal is solving your client's problems as well as your own. His problem was that he didn't know what to distribute effectively at the fair. My yardstick idea rendered a tremendous service. It was simple and straightforward, and it worked. It filled his need. I had simply built a better mousetrap by altering (cutting in half) an item that already existed. Subsequently, there were six repeat orders for 100,000 18-inch rulers.

All I did then, and all I do now, was to find a need and fill it—not by settling for the obvious need, but by using creativity and imagination to discover the *real* need.

Needs Around the World

When my company first went to Europe to manufacture and sell specialty advertising products we had one tremendous advantage: All the romantic stories we had developed and used in the United States until they were almost clichés were still brand-new in Europe.

Back in the 1950s I developed a very simple sales presentation. I would hand my business card to a prospective customer, then tell him to tear it up. He'd look at me, wondering about my sanity, but he'd do it. Then I would hand him a pen with my imprint on it: name, address, and phone number. "Break it in half," I'd say.

Now he had no doubts about my sanity. I was crazy. "Why should I break it? It's a good pen," he would say.

I made my point. He wouldn't break it because it had value. Even though it had an advertising pitch on it, he wanted to keep it. Advertising specialties get your message to people who will keep it. This was an old story in the United States, but when I told it in Europe it was fresh and new.

What did that teach me about trading overseas? I had all of the successes to work with and none of the failures! Since the rest of the world was then a few years behind the United States in terms of product development, marketing, and sales techniques, you could use all the successful U.S. ideas overseas.

People are people. Once you get past their initial cultural and nationalistic veneer, they are basically the same. They want to be prosperous, they want to eat, and they want to live, love, and laugh. And if you have found a way to reach people in the United States, use it in Germany and France and Japan.

Soon after I started my own specialty advertising business I went to San Francisco to market my ideas. San Francisco isn't too far from Los Angeles—just about 400 miles—but people there said to me, "That won't work here. It's okay for those fly-by-nights and jockeys in Los Angeles, but we're different here." But the techniques did work in San Francisco.

I decided to expand to New York. "Oh, no," people told me. "That may work on the West Coast, but here people are more sophisticated. It won't work." But the business worked in New York, too.

The same thing happened when I went into France. "That's okay for Americans. They're willing to try new things. They'll never go for it here in France." People went for it in a big way in France.

A good idea is a good idea is a good idea—anywhere in the modern world. It may not be a good idea in Biafra, but if it works in Los Angeles or New York, it will work in Rome and Copenhagen and Amsterdam and London.

There are many dramatic opportunities in the world today. For example, every country that has undergone deregulation of its major industries has experienced vast changes. In recent years the United States deregulated both banking and airlines, and the changes have been enormous. Today, in both England and France, they are going through the first phase of a similar deregulation. It is probably a trend that is going to sweep Europe in coming years, and it is a terrific opportunity, particularly for people who are already involved in those industries here. It reminds me of one of the oldest sales stories in the world. A guy was sent to Africa to sell shoes. He couldn't believe it and sent back a telegram saying, "This is ridiculous. I can't do it. Nobody wears shoes here!" The company brought him back and sent over another guy. After a couple of days, he sent a telegram back saying, "I can't believe it! The opportunity is unbelievable. Nobody has any shoes!"

Once people realize they have a need for shoes, who are they going to buy them from? The guy who has been selling shoes, of course. If the banks, airlines, steel companies, or automobile manufacturers of Europe are deregulated or denationalized, and if you understand what is going on, you can make a fortune. For instance, if you knew something about the banking business, you could go to France right now and sell the same bank promotions that have proved workable here. The French public has never seen them; it's a new story for them. You can present "original" (never before seen in France) promotions guaranteed to work.

The world has largely become homogenized—but not entirely. McDonald's may be all over the world, but all the other products, techniques, and processes we have to offer are not.

What's more, it's a two-way street for the international trader. Everything the world has to offer us hasn't been brought here yet, either. When you are in the international arena, you can play the game in both directions. You can find a need and fill it, anywhere in the world.

In 1956, when I first went to Japan, I discovered cloisonné. Asians have been doing this work for years, of course. Even then, you could find cloisonné in Chinatown in any major United States city. But the cloisonné in Chinatown was Oriental. What I grew interested in was translating that technique into something American. I would have cloisonné in a manner never seen before in the United States. I would bring the process over and convert it to American tastes and American needs.

My first deal was with Forest Lawn Mortuary in Los Angeles. I took a piece of cloisonné and wrapped it around a cigarette lighter. It was a depiction of the Forest Lawn statuary. It was terrific, and it worked. (But it shows how times change; today, with the connection between cigarette smoking and cancer, Forest Lawn would never put out a lighter as a promotional piece.)

We used the cloisonné technique for banks, oil companies, and other businesses by putting color pictures of their buildings on cigarette lighters. It was quite a revolutionary and successful promotion at the time. Today, we are updating it further. The Chinese produce cloisonné of outstanding quality, so we are negotiating to have Pierre Cardin design the graphics for writing instruments which will be reproduced in Chinese cloisonné. When production takes place, it will be an American pen with a French design done in Chinese Cloisonné—truly an international product.

Whether trading domestically or internationally, the process is the same. You find a need and fill it, or you have a product and you sell it where it is needed. The only difference is that on an international scope you radically enlarge the size of your marketplace. People believe that international trade must be more competitive, but just the reverse is true. Competition in the world market is much lighter because most people are afraid of it.

Being either an importer or exporter exclusively can be dangerous in today's world of fluctuating currencies, volatile economies, and changing social conditions. The international trader takes advantages of opportunities without limiting himself to a single role.

Getting Started

How can you get started in international trade? You see the necessity and the opportunity, but you don't know where to begin. The choices might even seem overwhelming to you. After all, there's a big world out there.

Begin with what you have. If you already have a business, find a need for that business. If you manufacture products, find a need for those products—or some variation of them. It's the path of least resistance, which is always the easiest.

If you are not in business and want to trade internationally, especially if you are young and starting out, get a job in a related field. I'm a strong believer in apprenticeships. It's very rare for someone to get a hit the first time up at bat. If you learn something about the business on someone else's time, and render a service in return, you have somewhere to start. When you are ready to go out on your own, you'll have some experience and judgment. You're liable to make fewer errors and suffer less pain.

But suppose you are already in business or have completed your apprenticeship and now want to enter the international arena as an entrepreneur. If you are already involved in a particular industry or have knowledge of it, go to that industry. Trade associations exist all over the modern world, whether for dollmakers, clockmakers, automobile manufacturers, specialty advertisers, electronics producers, or makers of general merchandise. These associations are a wealth of information on distributors, customers, and existing sales patterns. Closely allied with these are the foreign trade divisions of your local chambers of commerce and of your bank, if it has any stature at all. Yet another source of information are the trade divisions of foreign consulates in the United States. Read every book on international trade and get all the information you can on current transactions, all of which are a matter of record.

Based on your research, you will get a pretty good idea of how much your product or line of products is being imported, how much is being exported, and where it is being sold overseas. By the time you finish, at the very least you'll know who is buying and who is selling what.

Go to the international shows and fairs. You'll see what others are selling, what the prices are, what the distribution is. Probably 95 percent of what you see will be of no use to you, but you are looking for a niche to fit into, and the law of averages says you'll find it. Simply by asking, you'll discover firsthand if others can use what you have to sell or will sell you something you can use in the domestic market. What you do with the information depends upon you—your ingenuity, your experience, and your products.

Know Yourself

"Know thyself" is one of the oldest philosophical ideas on earth. And for good reason. It's as pertinent to business as it is to everyday life. In business, you have to know your strengths and limitations, how far to go and how far not to go, what risks you are comfortable with, and when not to take them.

People can be divided quite broadly into two groups: those who yearn for security and those who enjoy, even thrive, on taking risks. It starts early. There are just so many students at the top of the class; most belong to the vast middle group. At the outset of his or her career, a young person decides whether to be risk-oriented or to play it safe. The majority play it safe. This is not to demean one or the other, but it seems to be how we emerge as personalities.

It is not even a question of talent. A student can be very talented with figures and go into accounting, an honorable profession. He's willing to settle for a ceiling on his income in exchange for security; he knows he can always be employed as an accountant. A salesman, a trader, someone involved in marketing, a writer, or a painter has no such security. If he succeeds, he can make a great deal of money; if not, he can starve.

The real entrepreneur is driven to do what he does. He likes what he does; he can't work from 9 to 5. On the other end of the spectrum, those reliable people who form the backbone of our industrial societies could not live at an entrepreneur's mad pace, with all that unpredictability.

Pay attention to whom you are. Be whomever you are, and be it well. There's no disgrace and no great honor to be one rather than the other. The honor is in the degree of success you reach in your own estimation. A magnificent carpenter can gain the same satisfaction as a billionaire industrialist. It depends upon the individual.

The object of the game is not to amass tremendous fortunes; it is to fulfill whatever desire you have. Many times I've heard people (particularly wealthy, successful people) say, "Money isn't important. It's the scorecard." Bullshit! Money is important, and if that's their scorecard, that's fine. But it isn't the *only* scorecard. I know some very unhappy wealthy people. The scorecard is in your head.

Albert Einstein did not have the same scorecard I have. Neither did Vincent van Gogh. We all march to the beat of different drummers, which is one of the important factors that create the vitality and fascination of life. Knowing yourself *is* important. It probably underlies everything else. Know your stamina, your risk-acceptance level, your interests and skills, and your ability to develop new skills. If you can't stomach the thought of risk, don't become an entrepreneur. If you don't relish the safety and security of a 9-to-5 job, don't take one.

Make no mistake. The entrepreneurship of international trade involves risks. But it also involves rewards. You can make errors and lose money, but you can also win—and win big. If, like me, you are moved by the entrepreneurial spirit enough to act, I guarantee you'll be embarking on one of the greatest and most satisfying adventures of your life.

2

Opportunity International

I began my business career not as a global entrepreneur, but as a salesman. I suppose I'm still a salesman, but now I operate on an international level, as chairman and president of a large company. The basics of my business remain the same; I have simply extended my distribution to points beyond my city, my state, my country. In doing so, I have rid myself of a major limitation—the size of my market.

After early experiences with my brother, during which time we exported to China and India, I formed my own specialty advertising business and concentrated on importing for domestic markets. I reentered the export business almost by accident. In defense of my business acumen, however, I must add that when opportunity presented itself I grasped it with zeal. Let's overlook the fact that I had to have the foreign trade opportunity literally shoved in my face before I recognized a need I could fill.

It happened in Milan in 1970. Our company had been importing merchandise from Europe and the Orient since 1956. We had heard about the gigantic Milan Trade Fair and decided to go there. My intention wasn't really to buy or sell, but primarily to investigate. There were some fine products coming from Europe, and I wanted to see if there were any concepts we could adapt. Our business was specialty advertising, and we owned Everlast Pen Company in New York. We made a good product, but business was slipping. We competed with nearly 30 other United States makers of essentially the same pens. And the strong dollar brought further competition from abroad.

In 1970, however, the dollar began to weaken against foreign currencies, and opportunities for export opened up. I didn't see them. Involved as I was in the daily details of running a business, I couldn't "see the forest for the trees." Even though I had done some exporting during the early years, the thinking patterns that I had developed over time didn't include the concept of export.

The Milan Trade Fair is one of the largest of its kind in the world, covering miles of the city and exhibiting everything from heavy industry to small novelties. In 1970, an entire building was devoted to writing instruments.

I was particularly interested in seeing the novelty pens of low-priced manufacturers from Turin, near Milan. There had been some great successes in the retail market, and the products were worth investigating for the specialty business. It was April and very cold. As often happens in Italy, some labor union was on strike, and the heating system in this particular building wasn't operating. It didn't stop the show, but it certainly made it uncomfortable.

I entered one of the larger display rooms and saw, pacing up and down, a thin, balding gentleman of slightly autocratic appearance. In spite of his full-length camel coat, he was shivering slightly. He introduced himself as Albert Lucky, export manager for Farr of Italy, one of the world's largest manufacturers of novelty pens. The particular line that interested me was a plastic series in the shape of spoons, knives, forks, and other utilitarian products. When opened, they were actually ballpoint pens.

As we talked, I grew impressed by Mr. Lucky's knowledge of the pen business, and I told him something of what we did in the United States. He asked to see the most popular pen we manufactured. I showed him an all-metal pen with a gold

Florentine finish. The basic metal was brass, giving it a good, heavy feel and an expensive look. He asked me the price.

"About fifteen cents each," I said.

"Fifty cents," he said, nodding.

"No. *Fifteen* cents," I repeated.

Albert Lucky grew excited. "Fifteen cents each?" he said incredulously. "That's tremendous. I could sell millions of them!"

Now I had been in business for a few years by then, and I'd heard "We could sell millions!" a number of times. I certainly wasn't selling many millions in the United States. Still, this man did appear to know his business, and I felt it wouldn't hurt to discuss it further.

He asked if I would be interested in having him represent Everlast Pen in Europe. "How many can you actually sell?" I asked, getting to the key question.

Mr. Lucky thought for a moment, then said, "Well, I would have no problem selling at least two million dollars in the first year." Since Everlast Pen was doing a total business of one million dollars—and losing money at that—I had very little to lose.

Albert Lucky was a man of his word. He sold millions of pens in the foreign markets. What had been merely one of many similar products in the United States became a unique product abroad, because the same manufacturing and finishing techniques were not available there. Shifting exchange rates that I had barely noticed made it a viable product for export. The dollar was weakening, which made the European prices lower.

Was this simply luck? I don't really think so. The deal was made a reality through the factors of *need, timing, flexibility*.

I've already discussed need. Timing and flexibility are the effective responses to a need. Timing involves understanding today's market and acting on that understanding. Flexibility allows a salesperson who has always dealt with the same buyers to say, "There are probably other outlets, fresher markets. Let me find them." It allows a buyer who has always bought from the same sources to say, "There must be untapped sources of material. Let me find them." This flexibility lets you rapidly respond to market changes such as shifting currency rates, new product lines, and the like.

I have about 700 employees, and, when asked why he or she is doing something a particular way, the worst thing any of them can say is, "We've always done it this way." That's the road to failure. An individual's success depends greatly on his or her ability to shed some of the parochial rules taught earlier in life. In fact, the major enemies of timing and flexibility are ego and habit. If the first Thou Shalt of trading is "find a need and fill it," the first Thou Shalt *Not* is don't "fall in love with your own ideas." The marketplace—particularly the international marketplace—is an expensive arena in which to flex your machismo. Blind commitment to a nonusable concept has led to many lost fortunes. A well-known example, of course, is Ford's expensive commitment to the Edsel automobile.

Hiding Your Head in the Sand

In today's competitive world, American business can no longer afford the luxuries of ego and habit—even though ego is reassuring and habit is comfortable. The solution to many of our current business woes—flat or shrinking domestic markets, lower profit margins, foreign competition—lies in ridding ourselves of these blinders. Ego and habit block vision and now, above all, vision is crucially needed. The stopgap measure of legislative protectionism is not visionary; ignoring the realities is not visionary; regulation is not visionary. Ready or not, the world is competing with us. We can no longer ignore this fact and remain economically viable.

Over the years, protective tariffs and other forms of regulation have proved detrimental to the economy and, ultimately, to the consumer. Not too long ago, a round-trip airline ticket from Los Angeles to New York cost $500 and up.

Because of airline-industry deregulation, a ticket can now cost as little as $100 each way, depending on circumstances. Though the inevitable shakeout occurred, the industry emerged far stronger and the consumer was a major winner.

All that keeps the price of merchandise in line—and all that has ever kept a lid on prices—is competition. Legislate competition out of existence and you have disaster. Without competition, the necessity for good management disappears, and the resulting cost increases are passed along to the consumer.

Remember Detroit? They once had a wonderful game going. Every now and then General Motors, Ford, and Chrysler sat down with the unions for a bargaining session. The unions demanded, the automakers conceded, and a new contract came into force. The auto companies added $2,000 to the price of a car: $1,500 to take care of union demands and another $500 to take care of their profits. What did they care? They had an enormous domestic market that had very little alternative but to buy their wares.

But nothing stays the same forever. The rest of the automotive world saw the need, and Volkswagen, Mercedes-Benz, Toyota, Datsun, and Honda attacked the U.S. market with vigor and creativity, attacking the bloated bureaucracy of the American automobile manufacturers with design, price, and quality. Detroit became relatively noncompetitive almost overnight.

It wasn't only the fault of the unions; management was equally, if not more, to blame. Management suffered from fixed ideas, arrogance, and greed. And they paid the price.

One has to wonder what would happen if there were enough political pressure next week to say, "Look, we want to save our jobs in Detroit and Flint. Let's keep all the foreign cars out of the market. Let's not export our jobs to Japan and Korea and Yugoslavia." Without competition, U.S. automakers would succumb to the same temptations they did in the past, and the American public would once again be the loser.

Full employment is not and cannot be the primary goal of business. It is purely a political goal. Business has to succeed on the merits of good economic sense. If it doesn't, you enter the mishmash of regulations, subsidies, higher taxes, and monopolies—all of which destroy competition. If left to its own devices, business sooner or later generally does what it has to do to survive.

The American textile industry is a good example. It started in New England, but because of unionism and certain other conditions it moved to the South. There was regional dislocation, but it did not bring about a national trauma. New Englanders were concerned, of course, but they relocated, created new industries, and today are enjoying a high-tech renaissance.

The same approach applies on a global scale. Today it may make more sense to buy textiles from Korea than from South Carolina. If so, South Carolinians will adapt and survive. The essence of international trade is to buy and sell where the process is best, not where politics dictates. A two-way stream of import and export ultimately creates as many jobs as are lost. It may not happen overnight, but it will happen through the natural flow of business, rather than by an artificial, usually expensive, attempt to keep people working. The result will be products that are actually needed and wanted, in a good economic balance.

In essence, regulation is an attempt to tell the American public what merchandise to buy and who to buy it from. And that's wrong. It's bad for the individual, for the country, and for the economy. With international trade, government's legitimate function is to negotiate decent trade treaties, so we are not placed at unfair disadvantage by varying degrees of protectionism overseas.

People around the world admire the United States. We have the highest standard of living in the history of the world, and most foreigners want what we have. They admire our technology and our style. And they want to trade with us. It is not a question of creating laws to keep them out, but a matter of saying, "Okay, come in and trade. We'll send you our things and you send us yours." If we do this with ingenuity, creativity, and aggressiveness, there is no question that we will dominate the international markets and bring about an unprecedented era of prosperity.

Looking Past Your Nose

Although you may not realize it, you are probably already involved in international trade. Do you have a Korean shirt, a Japanese car, shoes from Italy, or a wool sweater from England? If you are an average businessman, are your office machines from Taiwan or Tokyo? If you are a manufacturer, do some of your parts come from Asia or Europe?

These are all *imported* goods, hence our current trade imbalance. The true road to viability involves both import and export. All it takes is a new and more flexible way of thinking— a willingness to expand current markets without viewing international boundaries as barriers.

But old habits die hard. Most people are frightened by the very idea of export. It seems a complex and overwhelming task involving red tape, great distances, foreign languages, strange currencies, and lack of control. True, there are new complexities and nuances, but every business is complex and international trade is no more so.

Export becomes an attainable goal if regarded merely as an extension of your current distribution. If you manufacture a product in Los Angeles, you would think nothing of taking it to San Francisco. It's a little more frightening to take that product to Chicago or New York, but not enough to stop you if you have the desire. How much more frightening could it be to take your product to Europe?

Getting to foreign markets isn't nearly as difficult as it once was. The trailblazers have already laid the groundwork and better communications and mutual understandings exist today in the international marketplace. And business has become increasingly homogenized. These days the same hot products are available around the world. I recently tallied the products we sell in the United States and those we sell in Europe and Asia. The Number 1 product is the same worldwide, and the product I have difficulty selling domestically also gives me difficulty abroad.

The "mysteries" of international trade are not really all that mysterious. In this book, I hope to demystify them, strip away the nonessentials and technicalities, and present a clear picture of what is really involved. If I talked to you about bills of lading, sight drafts, and other details, it would probably be thoroughly confusing. But I don't have to do that. I've been involved in international trade for 40 years and I have never filled out a bill of lading or cleared a shipment personally. There are literally hundreds of technical specialists who will do that for you, for a reasonable fee. These are relatively unimportant details. There are far more important and basic factors involved in trading internationally.

At its roots, all business is concerned with seizing opportunities and solving problems. In 1970, I had a problem— a pen factory in New York that was overstocked with a product I had trouble moving. The opportunity was in Europe, where this item, common in the United States, happened to be new and unique. I not only solved my problem, but I filled a need in a foreign market. It was the best kind of deal—everyone got what they wanted and everyone made money.

I believe that the vast majority of products manufactured in the United States can be sold profitably in other parts of the world. We've all heard of the difficulties faced by garment workers in this country due to competition from inexpensive foreign labor. In spite of this, American blue jeans are still very much in demand around the world. Why? Because people in foreign countries don't want jeans with an Italian or a Japanese label. They want a label that says "Levi." In France, American designs have the same respect that Paris designs have in the United States. The factors involved in this preference are style consciousness and snobbery. Taking advantage of these factors is simply a matter of skillful marketing.

Another example involves the field of electronics. We discovered that Asian countries could manufacture these products for much less than we could because they have lower labor costs and this type of manufacturing is not heavily automated. The response of some American companies was either to sell the process to overseas manufacturers, or to find a trading partner in Asia and license him to make the product there. They did not abdicate because of the competition.

Other companies and industries have faced similar problems with overseas competition and have been able to export the end product of their highly automated assembly lines, where the higher cost of labor is compensated for with lower material costs.

There *is* a way to export your materials, your processes, or your knowledge. Potential customers in other countries are probably already looking for what you have to offer. It is simply a matter of finding the means of communication that will help them find you.

Where the Action Is

You can't hit a home run unless you keep swinging the bat. It's impossible if you're not in the game at all. Obviously, it's the same in business. You can't take advantage of an opportunity unless you've made yourself available in the marketplace.

Getting into the game calls for a new state of mind. It takes vision that sees across national boundaries and views the world as one vast market. It takes flexibility and willingness to reach further than you have reached before. Whether you actually travel or travel vicariously through magazines, trade publications, and correspondence, once you start this new way of thinking, the opportunities will present themselves, often unexpectedly.

In 1977, I attended a trade fair in Düsseldorf, West Germany, and a particular item attracted my attention. At first it looked like a solid block of material, perhaps plastic.

Advertising copy was screened along four sides of it, so that it looked like a cube with writing on each side. I wondered why on earth anyone would want it.

When I looked closer, I saw it was a tightly packed scratch pad with some 700 sheets of paper. People would keep it because it had a purpose. It was a simple item, but there had never been anything like it before. It presented an opportunity.

I ran through the options. I realized that you couldn't import paper economically: It's too heavy. If we took orders in Los Angeles, sent the advertising copy to Düsseldorf, and had them screen the copy on the sides of the pad and ship it back to us, the time factor would also be unworkable. It would have to be shipped by air, and the cost would be out of line.

There were no patents on the item; it was far too generic. Additionally, we had bought from that company before, and they knew it wasn't good business sense for us to buy this particular product from them. As soon as I returned to the United States I started looking for people with the technical ability to screen the sides of a note pad. It was difficult, but finally I found someone who could do it. With the quantities I wanted, however, he needed extra equipment, which would have involved a sizable investment.

Instead of giving up the idea, I went into a joint venture with the screener. I provided the extra equipment and, of course, the distribution. We sold millions of the item. In fact, we were so successful that a lot of people in the United States copied the idea. You've probably seen these pads in gift shops around the country. Part of my philosophy, however, is not to stay in a business that becomes too crowded. As soon as the bloom was off the rose, I sold out to our joint-venture partner for a very nominal price. I was soon out of the manufacturing end, and now I just buy from him when I need to.

This was an entirely unexpected and extremely lucrative result of a trip to Düsseldorf. When you are in the world marketplace you have eyes and ears to a whole arena of new products, processes, and opportunities. If you are not there, it is just not going to happen.

Why Trade?

Perhaps you think I've already answered the question, "Why trade?" Apart from opening up new business opportunities, however, there are other benefits. These include:

sales stability
increased competitiveness
expanded markets
increased sourcing for what you sell
greater profits
personal enrichment
international peace

Sales stability comes with increased distribution, which is, of course, one of the purposes of expanding into new export markets. The more distribution you have, the more insurance you have that your business will be prosperous. As has happened before, though there might be a recession in the United States, economies can still be performing well in other parts of the world. If United States demand for your product has lessened, the demand can still be fresh in other parts of the world. Finally, the more distribution you have, the better control you have over quality, manufacturing, and consistency.

International trade also increases your competitive edge. If you are importing, you have more choice of products and materials. If you are exporting, you are less dependent upon your regular channels. There is also a certain status to international trade, which can translate directly into increased sales. If you're a manufacturer who sells his products around the world, your salespeople can certainly command more attention by promoting that fact. There's nothing like saying, "We sell our products all over the world."

Sales stability, increased competitiveness, expanded markets, and increased sources for what you sell all add up to greater profits. If you already manufacture in the United States and you find an entirely new market overseas, the profit on incremental business is enormous. You already have your setups, you've already paid for your tooling, and your production line is already well organized. When you can add greater distribution to an already established manufacturing process your profits increase. Also, to cover the cost of export shipments you must have larger orders, which decrease your per-unit production cost.

Another important benefit is that if you handle your business properly through letters of credit and other conservative financial instruments there is no credit risk. I'll discuss this in more detail in Chapter 3, but the point is that generally you do not deliver on open account (ship now and collect later) when dealing overseas.

Finally, if you have established overseas trading partners, other U.S. business people who want to distribute their products internationally will flock to you with deals because you have already proved you can do it. Conversely, you can use your history of success to seek out opportunities among U.S. manufacturers and offer them overseas distribution. You'll often find you can make the deal because that business person is afraid to export; he doesn't understand the business and doesn't know what to do about it.

Finally, I can't say enough about the personal enrichment that comes with international trading. To meet wonderful people you might never otherwise have met, to experience new cultures, and to see places you might never have seen carry great rewards. I have been lucky enough to create long-lasting friendships in many countries, and through these people I have greater understanding and respect for their countries, their cultures, and their traditions. Whenever you meet your peer in a foreign country there is a wonderful search to know and understand each other. It is a valuable benefit that is promoted by free trade and destroyed by isolationism or protectionism.

Which brings me to perhaps the most important benefit of international trade. People who trade don't fight. In school I was taught that most wars were trade conflicts. The American Revolution had a strong foot in trade relationships. Japan's entry into World War II had much to do with the need to expand its trade in Asia and elsewhere. When people are barred from marketplaces through protectionism, they sometimes feel the necessity to force their way into the markets.

Now it's 1987, and although the Japanese lost that war, they have everything they wanted. They are winning the trade wars. And, interestingly, they have become totally pacifistic in the process. Preferring to concentrate on their consumer products, they resist the huge expenses involved in rearmament, in spite of persistent U.S. pressure. And they prosper.

There is no danger today of Japan fighting a war with any country. But there is a danger of the United States fighting a war. Who would we fight a war with? Our established trading partners—England, Japan, Germany, or Canada? No. We wouldn't fight any of the people who have the so-called favored-nations status for our import tariffs. Would we fight China? Probably not. It's a country in transition, moving from least-favored to most-favored trade status.

If we traded more with the Soviet Union, we would stand less and less chance of fighting them. We have much to offer each other, but instead both countries spend billions of dollars on ever-more-awesome weapons. I have heard people in Washington, D.C., say quite seriously that they know it's a strain on our economy, but it's a bigger strain on the Soviet economy. They're betting the Soviets will collapse first. The question is, why fight a war of attrition? Why not instead share all the advantages of our wonderful modern world through increased trade?

People who trade do not fight. It's as simple as that. You don't fight with your friends, nor do you fight with your trading partners. Trading partners meet, talk to each other, break bread. If you have a four- or five-day business meeting, you don't spend the entire time talking business. You talk about your children, your education, your life-style, your culture. You laugh and you have a good time together. You meet their friends and they meet your friends. And you find that some of the myths that surround different cultures and peoples start to evaporate. You often become close friends.

People who trade do not fight. People who trade grow prosperous.

3

Fear—And Other Barriers

I once read a story about some fishermen on a lake in Africa. They don't catch fish with lines and hooks. Utilizing the hot African sun, they use wooden slats to create shadows in the water. The fish see the shadows and flee. The fishermen move the slats, pushing the fish into shallow water so they can catch them easily. To the fish, these shadows—simply an absence of light—are as real as walls.

There are both real and imagined barriers that prevent Americans from entering the international arena. Most of them are merely the result of confronting the unfamiliar, proving the truism that ignorance and fear go hand in hand.

These barriers include such problems as financing and credit checks, political situations, foreign language, red tape, and customs requirements and duty. They are all, in their way, real. What is imaginary is their severity. Once knowledge is acquired, fear usually disappears. And once understood, most of these problems can easily be overcome.

All the fears can probably be boiled down to one word: *risk*. These risks are of mis-estimating unfamiliar markets, of not being in control of the deal because of great distances, of being taken advantage of in faraway countries by unscrupulous foreigners, and, ultimately, of losing money. But all business involves risks, and if you are smart, you can always minimize risk to an acceptable point—that is, the point at which risk is acceptable to you.

Personally, I'm never willing to take a 50-50 chance in business. That's the same as tossing a coin, and it's not acceptable. Almost invariably, however, you'll find that risk is in direct proportion to potential profit. The more money you can lose, the more you can make. As in all business, you have to find the balance you are comfortable with.

What you should know is that your exposure should be no greater in the international market than it is in the domestic market. And, as in domestic situations, various actions can be taken to lessen the risks—actions that I call "taking out insurance."

The Risks Involved

Let's take a closer look at exposure and risk. If you are a manufacturer exporting your product, exposure takes two main forms. The first involves money—collecting what is owed to you—and the second is the possibility your product will be handled badly and your market subsequently destroyed.

What would happen if you shipped open account to the wrong person, or if your trading partner shipped open account to the wrong people and they didn't pay? The only protection you have is the person's good credit, which may not be good at all. What if he had good credit but doesn't like some facet of the merchandise when it arrives? He sends you a telex saying he's deducting a certain percentage from what he owes you because he didn't like the color scheme or some other thing. In the United States you can haul him into court, but if your customer is in Tokyo, do you sue him there or sue him here? How expensive will it be to do so? Recourse in such a case has limited options.

What if you discovered a market for your product overseas, but the distributor murdered it through bad pricing, improper packaging, inefficient delivery, or a hundred other things that can be badly done? Suppose you have an elegant name brand and that distributor destroys the impact and reputation of the item by putting it into discount channels instead of boutiques and department stores? Or, suppose you are an importer, and you have opened a letter of credit, which was collected on the other side upon shipment. You later found the merchandise shoddy, or the parts bad, or that the device simply doesn't work. What recourse do you have?

These are all normal risks. They are magnified in the international marketplace, however, unless you know how to take out various insurance policies to protect yourself. These are not traditional policies that you write with an insurance company, but simply measures you take to protect yourself.

Ultimately, the purpose of insurance is to conquer fear. You have insurance on your house because you are afraid you will take a financial beating if it burns down. Insurance modifies that fear. The crucial element is how big your fear is and how much you're willing to spend. Although I live in California, for instance, I won't get earthquake insurance. It's a small amount of money, but it would be throwing it away because I have no fear of earthquakes and the risk is remote. These days, some insurance company somewhere will give you the odds against getting killed tomorrow. You can insure against everything—and spend a lot of money. Well, it's the same thing in business: the greater safety you want, the more insurance you have to pay.

The final decision is between the value of the product and the cost to you. All the insurance policies I take are as much a part of the cost of merchandise as the metal or other components that go into it. When I price an item, I include those costs. If I can make a profit on top of that, it makes sense.

Fear of the unknown is the worst fear of all. It is what keeps people from reaching beyond their present limits. Once you have quantified and qualified that so-called unknown, the fear diminishes. When you know what you are dealing with, then you can take the defensive actions that eliminate fear.

Before telling you about those actions, however, let's consider what happens when fears come true.

Our Escape from Turin

When adequate insurance isn't taken out to protect a business venture, the result can be disastrous, as it was for me once.

In 1972, our European agent Albert Lucky suggested we might be interested in manufacturing our American pens in Europe. Since we were having trouble delivering the product on time, it was worth considering.

The deal seemed to make sense. We had a good distributor in Turin, Italy, who along with Lucky would invest in the deal. We could buy the parts in New York, ship to Italy, and set up a small plant in Turin to assemble them. At the time, we were doing a good business importing the entire pen and paying 24 percent duty. By importing the parts, we would pay only 6 percent duty. In addition, we would have inventory in Italy and would be able to offer immediate delivery. From New York, we could offer only 60 days shipment. It was all very logical, and M.M.S. International was born.

We started losing money from day one. The unions were impossible to deal with and labor absenteeism averaged 20 percent per day. With a force of some 25 employees, there wasn't a day that 5 employees weren't missing.

The Italian government chipped in to make life miserable for us with some astounding rules and regulations. And they never failed to let us know when we were breaking them. One day, I was sitting in my Turin office—as cold as always— bleakly observing the less-than-modern set-up and my ragged, inefficient work force, when I received a call from an Italian bureaucrat.

"You are breaking the law," he informed me. I didn't know that losing money was breaking the law and, as far as I was concerned, that's all I was doing.

Not so. It seemed that under Italian labor law, if you operate a factory, at least 20 percent of your work force must be either war veterans or handicapped. It was 1972, and Italy's participation in World War II had ended with its surrender in 1943. Most Italian veterans were well over 65 years old. We had no choice but to comply. Our new employees included a couple of handicapped people who had a very difficult time making it from the desk to the bathroom.

But our main problem (one that we had completely overlooked) was that saboteur of all good intention, that nemesis of rational conduct: the Italian postal system.

The Italian post office was the most unpredictable, impossible government agency that has ever existed anywhere on earth. It was beyond understanding. The backlog of undelivered mail in our local post office was so great, they were forced to finally handle the problem. Did they hire more people? Did they work night and day to get caught up? No. They burned all the undelivered mail! Presto! The problem was solved.

We've all heard the story about the check in the mail. Half the people who owed us money said their checks were in that burned batch. But it happened all the time! What do you do when a distributor whose payment is late tells you that the check is in the Italian mail? You roll your eyes heavenward and wring your hands. What else can you do? Late mail, undelivered mail, lost mail, damaged mail, burned mail. You name it, we got it—or didn't. We never knew whether a letter would arrive in two days, two months, or two years.

All of this combined to make it virtually impossible to do business in a businesslike manner. To top it all off, the prime interest rate soared to over 20 percent, and we faced serious financial troubles. We had to make a move. What followed is what we now affectionately call our "Escape from Turin."

A year earlier, Singer Sewing Machine, a mile down the road, had tried to leave Italy. Immediately after they announced their move out of the country, the employees organized a sit-in. They allowed nothing to go out or come into the plant. I don't know how much Singer lost, but it was more than we could afford. Our move had to be more discreet.

We decided to steal our own factory. Albert Lucky and I planned the evacuation. We plotted it with the precision of a military operation. Two weeks before Departure Day we sent our most expensive and intricate machinery to Switzerland for repairs. Then we hired ten French longshoremen and rented ten trucks and buses. We took an option to lease another building across town in Turin so that, if necessary, we could say we were moving. And we were—to France.

The operation began on Christmas Eve, 1976. All the needed exit permits were presented at the very last minute, when Italian officials were stamping everything in sight in order to get home early for the holiday. At 6:00 P.M., the move started.

The packing was efficient and fast. But at 1:00 A.M., the Italian police descended on us, guns drawn. They thought a theft was in progress. We explained that it was our own factory and that we were simply moving across town.

"Why move on Christmas Eve?" the suspicious officers asked.

"We are very busy and have to start operations immediately after Christmas to fill our orders," we replied.

"Where are you moving to?" they asked, still suspicious.

We showed them the lease for the new location across town. That seemed to satisfy them and they allowed us to continue. We worked with increased zeal, and soon all the trucks were loaded. Under cover of darkness, the convoy set off. There were no major mishaps; we moved an entire factory out of Italy into the south of France.

It was as covert an operation as has ever been conducted in the history of American-Italian business. The next day, local newspaper headlines shouted that American capitalists had stolen their factory. It was not a popular move, but it saved our business.

It certainly wasn't a traditional, or even proper, way to move a factory. We would have preferred to do it according to the books. If we had, however, we would have suffered the same fate Singer had, without having the resources to offset that heavy loss. Our move didn't change employment in the area any more than if we stayed. The fact was that the plant would have closed down in any event. Long after the plant closed, we still honored old tax bills from the Italian government. Today I'm still welcome in Italy.

How did this travesty occur? Hindsight makes it simple. We didn't do adequate research beforehand to discover the problems we would encounter and, subsequently, we didn't take out insurance to nullify those problems. The unknown suddenly became known, and we weren't prepared for it. Our fears became realities.

Coping with Fear

We all have our pet fear; mine is to do business in a Third-World country. Italy is not in that category, and conditions have improved considerably, but it gave me a relatively benign taste of what could happen. I have a policy not to do business in underdeveloped countries. I have a real fear, and as I can't take out an insurance policy to cover that fear, I pass.

I don't consider this some subjective bias, but a rational fear based on my judgment of people and on the track record of their countries. The economic reality of the Third World is that the countries haven't performed. This does not influence my feelings about donating money to starving people. It has to do with my personal fear of doing business with people who don't have a track record, who aren't professional, or who are not work-oriented.

I put a lot of faith in work orientation. I can walk into a Swiss factory or a bank and agree on something on the basis of a handshake. Even without substantiating documents, I am confident the agreement will be executed. That's the top of the business scale. I can lower it a few degrees with each country. West Germany is just below that, England is below that, France is next, then Italy, and then Spain. By the time

I get to Saudi Arabia, Jordan, Mexico, or Ghana, they are so far down the line I don't want to touch them. There are no gold-plated and deliverable deals when you move that far down the scale.

Most developing countries these days have chosen a path of bureaucracy, rather than productivity. People who could be making shoes or processing food are instead shuffling pieces of paper. Those developing countries that have been successful, such as South Korea and Taiwan, have firmly supported free-enterprise systems. Unfortunately, when it comes to the Third World, they are a select minority.

When I'm seeking worldwide markets for a line of writing instruments, I know that buyers in France, West Germany, or Switzerland are only concerned with price, quality, and marketability. I can sell the product on its merits, with very little added complexity.

If, as I have done, I take the product line into the Middle East, I am suddenly faced with a jungle of government restrictions, and there is someone close to someone else who needs to be bribed.

Even worse things can happen. Once we struck a deal with a very enthusiastic distributor in a Middle Eastern country. He said he knew exactly where he could sell the product line, and indicated he would place an immediate order. Could we ship it? We specified the terms as a letter of credit. That would take some time, but it was no problem, he said.

But then the deal grew complex. He needed the goods immediately, but the letter of credit would hold things up. He proposed that we ship half the goods right away, then he'd have the letter of credit open to us within 30 days. He would give us a partial cash payment immediately. Against our better judgment, we accepted the cash and agreed. The merchandise was shipped and never paid for. The letter of credit was never opened.

We had several propositions from potential customers in Iran who would only buy a product if we invoiced them at 50 percent the actual price. They would pay that amount with a letter of credit and find some way of getting the cash to us for the remaining half. They did this because import duties were so high in Iran. If they bought $20,000 worth of a product and we invoiced them for $10,000, they would pay duty only on the $10,000. They promised that just before the shipment was due to go out, someone would get the cash to us.

It was an added complexity. Through the years, many promises were made and broken, many schedules were thrown off, and many times merchandise was made to order and never delivered. I don't want to do that kind of business. I want to offer a legitimate value to a legitimate customer. I've found that when I get involved with manipulations that have nothing to do with the product or business at hand, it diverts a lot of attention and energy and really isn't worth it.

I am in no way making a political judgment or an assessment of the worth of a country or its people. It is quite possible that if I were dealing with essential materials—food, clothing, or machinery—the situation would be different. But when dealing with a semiluxury item for which there is no absolute need and that needs a specific market, I cannot profitably sell my merchandise on a continuing basis in the Third World. Perhaps there is a lot of money to be made by trading in the Third World, but I don't know anyone who has made it. The reward-risk ratio is too lopsided. I don't feel the need to deal with Socialist bureaucracies, to face problems of corruption and bribery, or to contend with erupting revolutions. My method of coping with that fear is to pass on the opportunity, and that's my advice to others.

Insurance Options

I mentioned earlier that there are actions you can take to minimize your risks. In the pages that follow I discuss some of those possible actions.

Financing

How do you minimize your financial exposure? How can you be sure of collecting the money due you when you export?

The surest and easiest way is to open a letter of credit. This is done through your bank, where presumably you have a credit line or can establish one. As mentioned earlier, the bank essentially is giving you a credit line, which is only applied when the terms of the letter of credit are met. The bank that issues the letter of credit guarantees it and pays it.

Let's say you open a letter of credit in the favor of XYZ Company in Seoul, Korea. It's called a confirmed, irrevocable letter of credit. The beauty of it is that the letter can specify certain terms and conditions, such as a specific shipping date, bills of lading, proper market invoices, even inspection certificates that guarantee the quality of the merchandise. When all the terms are met, the vendor receives his money from the bank.

The letter of credit is an extremely valuable tool, since it handles the problems of credit risk, timely shipment, and merchandise quality. This is extremely inexpensive and efficient insurance, too. The fee charged by the bank is generally ¾ of 1 percent. Not much to pay for peace of mind.

There are many other financing tools available that can be tailored to your needs. For instance, you can use a bank draft. It is basically the same as a letter of credit except that you extend it by making it a 30- or 60-day draft. This is a means of financing by extending the payment, and the bank still guarantees it.

Once you know your trading partners well, you needn't bring a bank into it at all. Simply negotiate terms that are agreeable to both. Whatever your financing needs are, it is always possible to alleviate the risks involved.

Quality

You've imported shoes from Italy. When you saw them in Milan they looked wonderful, with fine stitching and top-of-the-line leather—not at all like the shoes the shipper delivered to Los Angeles. Your check has already been cashed, or your money wired, or your letter of credit collected. What recourse do you have? Very little, because you didn't take out any insurance.

There are a number of "policies" you could have applied. For example, you could have dealt through a trading company or an export broker. Or you could have hired an inspection company.

A trading company's business is trade. Generally, it manufactures nothing. It is a company that buys and sells merchandise according to the needs that it finds, usually on its own account. A reputable trading company possibly is your best alternative. Trade is its business, and it stands behind its merchandise. If goods are shoddy, you don't go to the manufacturer for restitution, but to the trading company because it is buying and selling on its own account. In effect, the trading company acts as if it were the manufacturer, but it trades in many different items.

It's interesting to note that the great economies of the world were established to some extent by trading companies. The Hudson's Bay Company had much to do with opening up North America. The British East India Company opened up Asia and India for the British Empire. The greatest recent examples are the Japanese companies.

These trading companies are 100 percent market driven, not product driven. They find a need and fill it. They are not married to any kind of product or to production in any particular place. There is nothing ethereal about the way they do business.

Another alternative is to use an export broker. His job is to act on your behalf, for a fee. he doesn't buy and sell for his own account, as a trading company does. He takes a commission varying from 1 to 10 percent for buying the product for you and looking after your interests.

Inspection companies are usually international in scope. Their business is to inspect merchandise on your behalf and give it a seal of approval. You set the standards, and they look for those things. If the product passes muster, they provide an inspection certificate. If this is one of the terms of your letter of credit, the manufacturer cannot collect until the inspection certificate is provided.

Finally, another more expensive and generally unnecessary alternative is to travel to the country and inspect the merchandise yourself before it is shipped. If you are doing business in Europe or Asia, however, there are many resources that render this unnecessary. Whether you deal through a trading company, an export broker, an inspection company, or some combination of the three, you are usually well protected.

Checking References

You've established communication with someone overseas regarding either import or export. Are you dealing with a liar and a thief? How do you find out?

Credit and reputation are checked most easily through the other party's bank. Most experienced overseas business people realize this, and in their first letter to you they usually say, "For references, please contact Mr. Joe Jones at the Bank of England." They make it easy for you, providing an address and a telephone and telex number.

You can also use trade sources, provided through embassies, consulates, and even chambers of commerce. But this takes longer and requires patience. If you want to go a step further, ask the person for names of people he has done business with in the United States and call the companies involved.

You can check on anyone, almost any place in the modern trading world. If he has done business he is visible, either through his bank, his suppliers, or his customers. The reputation of the person with whom you are doing business should be of real concern to you, but it is easily handled.

Here's a clue that should alert you to what kind of person you are dealing with. If you call or write and ask for credit and reputation references, the person should say, "Sure, I understand. Call the Bank of —— and speak to ——." He should understand your needs and concerns; a good supplier or trading partner will give you all the references you want.

But if the person acts as if you have just insulted his mother, his family lineage, and his country, beware. You could be heading for trouble.

International Conditions

This fear could be summed up by saying, "don't do business in Lebanon because they blow up more things than they produce." But that would be glib. We live in a volatile world, and fluctuating conditions are of real concern. It is of far less concern to me than to some people, however, because I don't deal in Third-World countries, which tend to be politically and socially more unstable.

Some American companies choose to stay in places such as Libya. But their people get combat pay, and the company makes combat profits. When I was a Second Lieutenant in the U.S. Air Force, the standard salary was $150 a month. If someone was a flying officer, he got 50 percent more flight pay; if he were in combat, he got another 50 percent on top of that. The same thing happens in business. A businessman is a fool if he takes more risk and doesn't get more profit from it.

There are plenty of stable countries in the world. About the only thing you can't avoid entirely is the modern illness of terrorism. It is unlikely to affect your products, however, unless you happen to be standing in a French market when a bomb goes off. The odds are that you won't get hit by a truck or blown up by a terrorist bomb.

Foreign Language

This is a genuine but largely overrated fear. It is easy to protect yourself. If you speak the language of your trading partner or supplier *fluently*, you have no problem. The biggest problem is when you *think* you speak the language. If attempting the language, be extremely careful to ensure you are understood. When two Americans talk it's tough enough for each of them to leave knowing exactly what the other said.

You compound the potential problems by speaking a foreign language. The insertion of a negative, the use of an improper noun, or the misapplication of a colloquialism can take you 180 degrees in the wrong direction.

Today English is the international language of business. It is more than likely that the people you deal with will speak English. However, your best bet is to use an interpreter, even if you understand the foreign language. In fact, an interpreter gives you an added advantage in serious business discussions. You hear and understand the question, have time to think while the interpreter explains it to you, and then sound very clever by answering immediately.

It is wise to keep in mind, however, that whether using a professional interpreter or talking directly to a businessman who speaks English, it is a strange language for that person. You can go into a restaurant in Paris and find a waiter who speaks "perfect" English when he takes your order. However, ask him directions and he is suddenly stammering. He speaks restaurant English; that is all he is really familiar with. When dealing with foreigners, be wary of their limitations. It is always best to (a) speak slowly so that they understand you; and (b) keep the message brief, using as many small words as possible. This is no time to test your word power.

If you take the trouble to learn the language to some extent, submerge your ego and use it only during social occasions, not when talking serious business. When sitting down to dinner, give them all a good laugh with your mispronunciation of words. It's not wise to do it during business discussions.

Red Tape

This is another aspect of trade that has received bad press. The transfer of documents or merchandise may be complex, but it is really not your problem. Filling out export documents, shipping merchandise, clearing it through customs, and similar activities are all done for you, for a very modest fee, by various companies such as freight forwarders or shippers. The relatively light cost of the export broker, the shipper, or the freight forwarder should be included in the cost of your merchandise, of course. Only in very rare instances, such as when you are dealing with critical materials or with a hostile country, are export or import permits even needed.

In short, red tape is nothing to be afraid of. Not only is it minimal, but there are professionals to handle it for you.

Customs and Duty

Like death and taxes, customs duties are an unavoidable fact of life—and just as irritating.

Import duties can be very complicated. Customs departments have manuals the size of encyclopedias listing all the regulations. It's so complex because goods are subject to individual port-of-entry determination. You can have the same product come through New York, Boston, Los Angeles, and San Francisco and pay four different duty rates, depending entirely upon how each port classifies the merchandise. If you import a pen, for instance, it could be classified as stationery, a writing instrument, or a ballpoint pen. Each has a different duty rate.

We had a problem importing a unique key chain pen. Called the Courier, it was both key chain and pen. Which classification did it fall under? Both. We had to break it down and separately declare the cost of the key holder and the pen. Then they assessed it.

Nowhere is the face of protectionism more apparent than in our own tariff structure. The American cigarette lighter industry used to be protected by a 55 percent tariff on foreign imports. This was for the benefit of Zippo and Ronson. In 1950, Ronson was the second-best-known trademark in the world after Coca-Cola. In spite of protective tariffs, today it is all but out of business. Politicians and lobbyists claim that protective tariffs are there to keep us in business. It's not true. Good business keeps us in business. Good production, better products, keeping up with the times—those factors keep us in business, not protectionism.

A recent example of this was a union move to limit the use of imported parts in automobiles. There are very few products today that don't have some foreign pieces. Certain things just doesn't make economic sense for us to produce. Every time government (or special interests through government) uses duty or tariffs in an apparently well-meaning effort to preserve jobs, it creates ten more problems, particularly for those involved in international business.

Customs is an enormous bureacracy, and it follows that duties are thus enormously complex, particularly if they involve a complex item and the classification is in question. The saving grace is that, under normal circumstances, you don't have to deal with the question of duties. All you do is call your freight broker and ask him what the duty is on a particular item. He'll tell you, because that's his job.

In summary, it is easy to contend with the common barriers that prevent American businessmen from expanding beyond their borders. Whether your business is in the merchandising or service sector, when you expand overseas you are simply extending your distribution lines or expanding your market. It is no more complex than that. The business basics apply, particularly the rule of finding a need and filling it.

The best edge is an understanding of the marketplace. Like most things in life, trade operates under both fixed and variable laws. Once you understand the rules and their exceptions, you can do away with many of the confusions and cut a clear path for yourself. Overcome lack of adaptability, ingenuity, imagination, and foresight. America has had, after all, the greatest gathering of pioneers and innovators ever assembled in one country. We have to rekindle that spirit of adventure and opportunism. Reach out. A world is waiting.

4

How to Buy and Sell

If you want to build a house, you don't do it all yourself. Nor do you hire the plumber, the carpenter, the architect, the cement maker, the bricklayer, or the laborers. No, you go to a contractor, who gives you a price for the entire package. In business, if you know the technique of trading, you are that contractor. Your place in the market is to put the deal together so it solves everyone's problems, with the seller selling more, the buyer buying more, and the consumer consuming more.

The technique of trading must be rooted in knowledge. It takes creativity and integrity. You do not act as a "finder," with no meaning or production value. To trade well, you must perform vital functions that do not unnecessarily elevate the cost of the merchandise or eat up someone else's profits.

Furthermore, trading is based on the underlying knowledge that the deal is more important than the product. Where is the opportunity? Is it to buy, sell, lease, license, or enter into a joint venture? What is the product? At what price can you make or buy it? Where can you sell it and at what price? Those are the elements that form the concept of the deal.

My success in setting up businesses around the world has not occurred through an understanding of the details involved, but from knowledge of the markets and the techniques of trading. Business success rarely comes from being a visionary; it results from the ability to assess the market six months to a year ahead.

To do this, you need trading partners around the world. Doing business with many different types of people expands your customer base as well as your sources of supply and your inspiration. It also allows you the best of both worlds—to be both importer and exporter.

Options are important to the trader. There is much in the marketplace that you are not large enough to influence. For example, you have little or nothing to say about interest rates, currency fluctuations, import tariffs, and other government regulations. All you can really do is recognize the conditions that exist and react accordingly. The more one-dimensional you are, however, the more you are subject to market fluctuations.

In today's volatile business climate you must have the ability, and be willing, to change. If your main business is exporting, for instance, and suddenly the dollar strengthens against foreign currencies, it may become almost impossible to remain competitive in foreign markets. But suppose you are in the export and import business. Suddenly, you have a great deal more latitude. If the dollar is strong, you import; if it is weak, you export.

Your most important asset, however, is knowing *how* to trade. The technique of trading is more important than the product. Some people might not agree, but let me explain.

You can always find products; there is no shortage. But products come and go—they are transient. It is trading technique, however, that brings the products to market. And the technique stays with you. Once you master the basic principles of trading and deal making, you can use them for as long as you wish.

Trading is the method you use to set the most direct, economical route from manufacturer to consumer. It involves boiling the deal down to its most basic structure. And what is that basic structure? Whenever you approach someone with a deal, he always asks one main question: "What's in it for me?" That's the question you have to answer. Give him more business, give him greater profit, give him something he didn't have before, and you have set your position in the market.

That, in essence, is the technique of trading. It requires simply being there and doing a great job.

Putting Yourself in the Picture

There are three parties to any deal: the person who makes the item, the person who sells it, and the person who buys it. Maker, seller, buyer. As a trader, you insert yourself into this picture by performing a valuable function.

Sometimes the maker and the seller are the same person, but it is rare to find a good maker who is also a good seller. These are activities that require different skills and resources, and very few people can shift back and forth from technical expert to creative salesperson.

One of my favorite stories involves a portfolio we once designed. I was visiting Hardy Harvey, a close friend and business associate who lived in Waco, Texas. He was selling a product that I thought was terrific. It was a 4 × 8 inch bank bag made of a quality reinforced vinyl with the feel of good leather, yet it was just a little more expensive than ordinary vinyl. Just about every bank in Texas was distributing these imprinted bags to merchants, who used them to transport their cash deposits to the bank.

Harvey thought I'd be able to sell a ton of bank bags, but I didn't feel there was a market for them in Los Angeles. It was a neat item though, and I knew there was a market in L.A. for portfolio cases. I asked Hardy if he thought the maker could create a portfolio out of the same material.

"Let's go ask him," he said. The maker's name was Earl. He was a fifth-generation Texan, who also lived in Waco.

"Earl, can you make a portfolio out of this material?" Harvey asked.

"No, sir," Earl said earnestly. "I only make bank bags."

Hardy looked at me, and then at Earl for a long moment. He cleared his throat. "Tell you what, Earl," he said. "Can you make a bigger bank bag, like about 11½ × 16 inches?"

"Why, sure. I can do that," Earl replied cheerfully.

Hardy took me aside and said very seriously, "Don't never tell ol' Earl he's making portfolios, you hear. He can only make it if he thinks it's a bank bag." Earl made the "bank bags," and we sold hundreds of thousands of his portfolios.

Trading technique boils down to a gut-level understanding of the buyer's needs. Generally, the manufacturer doesn't understand this; it's up to the trader. The trader must possess extraordinary knowledge of the particular subject. After all, he has to pull off a miracle by demonstrating the unbelievable capacity to satisfy everyone's needs in a deal.

As liaison between buyer and seller, the trader has to know the problems and needs of both buyer and seller, and fill them. This is not just being a go-between—someone who introduces buyers to sellers and then pockets a finder's fee. The trader will commit to buy, design, or set up distribution, or some combination of these functions.

For a trader, the crucial question is what position you'll take. What are you equipped to do? How much are you willing to invest in time, facilities, and money? An underlying aspect of all of this is knowing who you are—being able to recognize your abilities and play to your strengths. When I first entered the advertising specialty business it was referred to as advertising novelties and calendars. The biggest part of the business was calendars. I started my business knowing I couldn't afford to sell calendars. I couldn't compete. First, there was one major company that absolutely controlled the business; they had a better product, better distribution, better everything. Second, salesmen who sold calendars had to be paid their commissions when they sold them. If they sold calendars in January or February for the following year, however, you had to wait a full year before you got *your* money. I couldn't afford the competition or to float that much money.

I had to determine my strengths and weaknesses. My strength was versatility. I didn't have to move a mountain to change a company policy. I could deal more directly with customers' problems and provide faster service. So I played to that strength rather than try to beat the master at his game.

I started to sell what I called "ideas that mean business right now." If someone said to me, "Aren't you in the same business as Brown & Bigelow?" (the leader in the calendar field), I'd reply, "No, they're in the same type of business, but they sell calendars and remembrance advertising. If you want remembrance advertising, go to them. They're perfect. But if you want an idea that'll bring business in the door tomorrow, that's what I sell."

There are two types of fighters: sluggers and boxers. The worst thing for a boxer to do is to slug it out with the slugger; he'd get killed. The worst thing for the slugger is to box the boxer. In other words, you have to go to your strength and do it faster and harder than the next fellow. Any game you get into has to be your game.

In international business, the playing field is so much larger. The options to enter the game at your point of choice are numerous. But whatever the role you set for yourself, the key is to become an absolutely vital part of the deal—the source of its success.

Making Deals

Before you come to a deal, you have to know the facts; you have to qualify it. Unfortunately, many people establish the conclusion first, then they rationalize the means to make that conclusion right. They start with the answer and come up with the questions. Wrong.

You have to start at the beginning. Once you completely understand the problems involved in a particular deal, they are half resolved. But if you don't understand them at all, you don't have a chance.

Closely related to this is the decision whether to have a product-driven or market-driven business. I strongly believe that traders and entrepreneurs should be market driven. A production-driven person says, "I've got a product and I've got to sell it." Mentally, he has a conclusion and has to prove it. A market-driven business person finds out what the market really wants and lets it determine his direction. In other words, he finds out what the need is and then fills it.

This theory applies in both product and thought processes. You have to be disciplined enough to seek out the facts and accept them. I know many people who not only won't accept the facts, but start to discredit the carrier of the facts. This is the "kill the messenger school," and it's an attitude that can get you into a lot of trouble.

You often find this situation in conflicts between accounting personnel and salespeople. Sales asserts the figures are right, and accounting says they are wrong. But accounting is based on an exact science; 2 and 2 never make 5. Sales is not as precise, and no matter how hyped up those people become, they should never discount the facts. You have to start with the right premise. If you have the right premise, you have a shot at coming to the right conclusion. If you start with an incorrect premise, your conclusion is invariably incorrect, no matter how brilliant you are along the way.

The above principle is about all I got from a course in logic at Columbia University. But throughout my business life, I have never forgotten it. If the premise is incorrect, you can draw ten "correct" conclusions, but the *entire statement* is false. Get the facts to make an informed judgment.

This lesson is often brought home to me in my business. When you are in the marketplace your reasoning ability is continually tested. My company once exhibited at various banking conventions, where we sold numerous promotional items. We had done particularly well at a national bank show, so the salesman in charge of our exhibit very enthusiastically said, "This was so great, I'd like to exhibit in the Texas show next."

"That's just a state show," I said. "It doesn't seem likely that we'd even cover our traveling expenses from Los Angeles."

"Our customers are there," he said. "Over 50 percent of our business at the national show came from Texas."

Well, that seemed to make sense. I could have accepted it and agreed to go to Texas. But I would have been flushing a lot of money down the toilet. Instead, I examined all the orders myself. Nowhere near 50 percent of the business came from Texas; actually, it was only 10 percent. I quickly put a stop to the plan.

The man hadn't consciously lied to me. He just hadn't examined the facts very closely. Maybe the Texas banks made a lot of noise, or perhaps the single largest order was from a Texas bank, or it's possible the prettiest women worked for the Texas banks. Whatever the reason, the Texas banks had made such an impression on this salesman that he *assumed* the majority of business came from these banks. If I had accepted his statements as facts, we would have lost a great deal of money.

In our complex world it is increasingly difficult to get the facts right. You can read statistics a hundred different ways, and often you have to look beyond the figures to the underlying causes. What created those figures? Why were they this way and not that way? Recognizing the facts of a situation is absolutely crucial to making rational judgments. And this is especially critical in making deals. You will have to put yourself in the other person's shoes; to do that, you must have knowledge.

Getting the facts of a deal involves knowing the other party's problems and limitations, who he has done business with, and how that business arrangement turned out. If you are dealing with a manufacturer, either at home or overseas, know what his capacity really is, what his profit structure is, and how his current distribution works. Then you can carve out a deal by working to *his* need, not to yours. Once you discover his real need, you can fit yourself into the deal by serving that need.

How do you find out about seemingly confidential facts such as the profit structure of a business? *Simply by asking.* You'd be amazed at how much people are willing to tell when you ask about their business.

I discovered this remarkable fact early in my career. I was selling merchandise that was to be given away as a promotion. Thousands of items were at my disposal, but what could I sell? If I approached someone in the automotive business and said I was selling pens or ashtrays, he wouldn't give a hoot. I couldn't intelligently present an item; I had to present an idea. But how could I come up with an idea that would help a man's business if I didn't know what his business was?

My tactic was to make an appointment with the president, marketing manager, or sales manager of the company. I'd tell him what business I was in and how creative we were, and I'd ask for just 15 minutes to uncover something about what he did. As a result, I would build a custom program for him and present it. If he liked it and it worked, he would buy it; if not, we would shake hands and say good-bye. No obligation.

I was amazed at the interviews. There were almost no boundaries set. All I had to do was ask some questions, "How much business do you do? Whom do you do it with? Where is your greatest success? What are your best products? What are your gross sales? What is your biggest problem? Have you sold overseas?"

Invariably, they would answer. Most people love to talk about their businesses and what they are doing. By the time I had that information, I knew exactly whom I was dealing with. I had acquired the facts needed to present a workable deal and found my spot in the market.

As mentioned earlier, finding your place in the market depends not only on your knowledge of the facts, but on having a realistic appraisal of your strengths. Once you know those factors you can come up with a workable plan that enables the maker to do more business than he could have done without you.

Export and Import Scenarios

Rather than speak in general terms, let's look at both importing and exporting, and the various alternatives available to the deal maker. For example, suppose you want to get involved in exporting. Suppose also that you haven't got a lot of money to invest or a great sales force. All you really have is an original idea or knowledge of a particular product or line of business.

If you have a track record, the first and most obvious thing is to act as a consultant. Sometimes I attribute to consultants what is often said about teachers: if you can't do it, consult. But that's unfair. Consulting can be a valid position, and a good consultant can show the neophyte the path through the jungle. A U.S. manufacturer that doesn't know how to go into the export business can hire a consultant. A manufacturer in Europe that wants outlets in the United States might do the same thing. But keep in mind that consulting is the least lucrative position to take in a deal

The essence of making a deal is to be *part* of the deal. It's buying and selling and taking a position. In accordance with the rules of business, the stronger a position you take, the greater the reward. Your investment can be in terms of time, facilities, money, or knowledge, but you have to make an investment if you want a significant slice of the pie.

Returning to our example of a manufacturer in the United States that would like to sell overseas—in Europe, for instance—let's consider a typical scenario. As deal maker you could become his export agent—an export distributor. The manufacturer has all his U.S. territories under control, but he'd like to expand overseas on a no-risk basis. An entrepreneur could solve this manufacturer's problem by saying, "I'll be your distributor for all your export business. I'll buy and I'll sell, and you'll have no problem. Just sell the goods to me here. I'll arrange for the shipments and all those other details that scare you so, and I'll pay you domestically. You send me a bill, and I'll send you a check."

That's one good position to take—*if* you have the outlets and can perform those functions. It doesn't necessarily mean you have the problem of stocking the merchandise; you can take the position without doing that. The key, of course, is to sell before you buy. If you have the outlets overseas or can find them, send out your offers. It's basically what I did in my very first experience with the blue serge for China. I acted as the principal, buying the material and selling it. But I didn't buy it until I had already sold it.

A word of caution. Once you make your offer in the marketplace you must ensure it will stick. Whatever deal you make, immediately confirm it in writing. If you don't know the person with whom you are doing business, go a step further and ask that individual to sign and return your letter stating the deal. This is everyday business practice that every businessman should do automatically, but 50 percent don't. Confirm even the simplest deal. Your letter of confirmation should summarize the deal:

> I agree that I will buy the product at $1 a piece, with the understanding that I will buy a minimum of 50,000 pieces, and I'll use them within six months. Please treat this as an option for 30 days, and it's up to me to exercise the option.

With such a confirmation you know you have the merchandise, you know the price, and you can offer it out and do your sales job and get your responses.

In this case, you are buying and selling, taking a full principal's markup on the item without much risk. You are not stocking the item. You don't even bring it to your warehouse (which is particularly handy if you don't have one). You arrange for your shipper to pick up the item at the factory and deliver it to the dock. This is one viable position, with a full range of variations ranging from acting as a broker or agent to simply getting a commission.

Now let's consider an entrepreneur wanting to import. For example, if you are starting out fresh, without the huge resources needed to import a whole line of products but interested in importing certain specialty products, then first you would go shopping overseas and make your decision on the products. You would go to a foreign manufacturer and offer to sell its product in the United States.

The manufacturer will say, "How many will you buy?" That's always the first question.

"Well," you say, "I'm not going to buy any to begin with, but I've got terrific distribution in the United States, and what I would like to do is. . . ."

And this is where the variables of dealing enter into the picture. The weakest position is to be an agent. The manufacturer has to worry about who you are and about the possibility of paying you an advance or paying your expenses, or what the market is really like. Instead, your best approach is to insert yourself into the deal in some way. For example, here are your options:

1. You have a lot of money you are willing to risk, so you buy right away and get exclusive distribution.
2. You don't have a lot of money, but you negotiate to take a 30-, 60-, or 90-day option, saying, "If I sell X amount, I will become your exclusive distributor in the United States." You gear your real ability to make money to your performance. This option isn't particularly frightening to the manufacturer. It has no distribution in the United States, anyway. The manufacturer has no intention of traveling to the United States and selling his product. As importer, you are offering to do it all, at no risk. That's a compatible deal
3. You can't get an option, but you like the product and think you can do the job on a nonexclusive basis. You take the samples, call on your customers, and book orders. Then you place the orders with the manufacturer.
4. You make a deal to represent the manufacturer. You sell the product at the cheapest price possible, take zero risk, and live on the commissions. This is the least desirable option.

As an import entrepreneur, these are your options, depending on the product, what kind of operation you have, what type of operation the manufacturer has, and your individual ability.

Deal making takes many forms, but the basics are the same. You make it easy for the other fellow to say yes. You make sure you offer a deal in which everyone wins. Business is often cast as a dog-eat-dog affair. That attitude has never worked for me, or for anyone I know. The reality of business is making deals that are mutually beneficial. Anyone who thinks of business as a cold, calculating activity gets exactly that out of it. Business only works when everyone—manufacturer on down to consumer—gets a fair shake.

When I was starting out, one of my best accounts was a lingerie company. The owner was a very nice guy, except that he tried to get everything at a bargain price. At the outset, when I needed the business, he would beat me down and I had little choice but to accept it. His approach made me resentful. When I began to do better and didn't need the business as much, I stopped calling on him. One day he called. "Jack, why haven't you come in to see me?" he asked.

"Let me speak frankly," I said. "You are a pain in the ass. You beat me down, you don't allow me to make my livelihood, you cut my price so that there is little or no profit. I don't need to do that."

"You don't need the business?" he asked.

"Sure, I need all the business I can get, but I just don't need it enough to want to go through that."

"Aaw, come on down," he said.

I went to his office and he said, "Look, Jack, I got to tell you something. I bought other things, but no one ever comes up with anything as good as your ideas and concepts. Now I have a particular sales problem, and I want you to solve it."

We discussed his problem, and on the spot I created a program that involved the use of a giveaway. "How much is it?" he asked.

I told him. He couldn't help himself. "You can do better than that," he said.

"You're doing exactly the same thing," I said, and I started to pack my bag.

"Now wait a minute. Don't get mad," he said, holding up his hand. "Okay, okay. You've got your price."

The point of the story is not to illustrate uncompromising standards or sticking to your guns, or some high principles. It shows that when you have the intelligence to provide your customer with what he truly needs, he feels good about the deal—even if he is a tightwad.

A Deal Based on Need

Making deals is not always sealing an opportunity and grasping it. Sometimes it is creating an opportunity out of necessity— as happened to me.

When we established our business in Europe, we were manufacturing a number of inexpensive sales promotional products, including pens. After the fiasco in Italy and following our escape from Turin, we moved to the south of France. I had the feeling I'd just jumped from the frying pan into the fire.

Our facility was too large for our kind of business. The overhead was enormous, dwarfing the volume. Once more I was faced with losing money. I analyzed the situation and saw that the missing ingredient was a product line in the higher priced range, which could find a ready market. To give me a clue to what we would sell in Europe, I examined our successful U.S. products and thought of the Sheaffer Pen Company.

Two or three years earlier Sheaffer had come out with a pen called the No-Nonsense—a big, bulky, all-plastic ballpoint pen. The quality was good and the writing excellent, but it was basically an old style that must have caught a nostalgia craze. Whatever the reason, the pen was a very big seller. We were the biggest distributor in the United States, but I wondered if I could bring it to Europe.

It was a difficult proposition. Sheaffer already had exclusive distributors in every European country. On top of that, they had a factory and a warehouse in the United Kingdom.

How could I possibly take control of the No-Nonsense pen? It would be of value to me only if I had an exculsive.

I dug deeper and came up with some pertinent facts. First, those European distributors were selling very few of this particular pen. Second, their entire distribution on the Continent was at retail level. No quantities of any consequence were being sold as promotional gifts, except at the top of the line. Europeans traditionally bought expensive gifts, in contrast with the United States, where people were accustomed to relatively inexpensive giveaways.

The Sheaffer No-Nonsense pen became my target. It would be a difficult deal to pull off. Sheaffer was an international company, a division of Textron, with volume well in excess of $100 million a year. It had a recognizable international name, with outlets all over Europe. How could I persuade them that it would be in their interests to let me distribute the pen in Europe?

I made an appointment with Sheaffer's top executives in Fort Madison, Iowa. There was little delay, since I was one of their largest U.S. distributors. I began the meeting by complimenting them on the good job they were doing with the No-Nonsense pen, resulting in our great success with it. In doing so, of course, I was highlighting the fact that we were their biggest customer. And I told them of our operation in Europe. Perhaps I exaggerated a little when speaking of how much business and coverage we had. I didn't lie about the figures, but I did give them a slightly headier version than reality.

As we talked, I discovered that the European distributors didn't want to sell them. Because of the duty and other elements, they only wanted to sell the higher priced pens. "Our people absolutely refuse to sell it," the vice president of marketing said with exasperation in his voice.

This was apparently a real problem to him, but I had the solution.

I offered them outstanding distribution—in the millions. I said I would take responsibility, not only for the No-Nonsense pen, but for the entire bottom-rung plastic line. And I wouldn't interfere with current distribution. "My guarantee," I said, "is that no product I sell will ever reach the retail market. I'll sell it with advertising copy only."

They were interested. But then I came up with the caveat. "All I'll do is buy parts from you," I proposed. "I'll set up my own production and assemble the pens. You can take it right off the mold. You don't have to assemble, you don't have to worry about markdowns, you don't have to worry about discounts, you don't have to worry about shipping; you just have to supply the parts. We'll bring them in, assemble them, imprint them, and sell them."

It was a marvelous deal for them because it was all incremental sales (sales in addition to existing sales, with no additional expense). The tooling was there; the parts were there. All they had to do was double the cost of the parts and sell them to us. Not only that, but we would pick up the merchandise from their factory, and pay them on a regular basis. Their only concern was any infringement on deals they had with current distributors. They told us that they would look into it.

The deal didn't happen in ten minutes; it took six months. But it was too good for them to pass up. They straightened out the legal factors and approved the deal. We brought the pens over to Europe, doing the same promotions we had used in the United States, and we distributed throughout the Continent. It was a dramatic success. We sold millions and millions of the No-Nonsense pens in every European country.

The story illustrates a complete deal. The need this time was ours. We had to have a higher-priced, prestigious product, and we had to find a source of supply. Our choices were Cross, Parker, or Sheaffer. Our research showed that Cross and Parker had much better distribution in Europe, so the target was Sheaffer. Next, we had to persuade them that the deal was the best thing for them. The way to do this was to prove that all they would gain was profit. The deal was made first by satisfying our needs, then by understanding the marketplace, and finally by understanding and filling the supplier's need.

It completed the circle and resulted in a deal in which everyone came out a winner.

The Deal—A Philosophical Indulgence

From the outset, I have worked on the basis that there is enough leeway to allow profit for everyone. If there isn't, the concept has to be changed. Any deal unfairly weighted to one side just won't last. A contract is only as good as the people who make it. If it does not benefit each party, then the loser is going to find a way to get out of it. I have yet to see a contract that can keep that from happening.

Somewhere along the line people have gotten the idea that to be successful, you must outmaneuver the other guy— that you must make a strong, if not cutthroat, deal that places the odds in your favor. Well, the odds should be in your favor, but only through the deal itself and the business possibilities inherent in it. You don't have to cut anyone's throat to profit in business. A deal is only as good as the benefits to everyone involved. I believe this idea should be taught in business school, but it is rarely mentioned. Aspiring magnates should know well that morality and ethics breed success on a more permanent basis than any other method.

5

Products

When it comes to choosing a product there's always a lot of pressure. Money, time, energy, reputation, and a dozen other factors are on the line. And, as we all know, nobody is right all the time. The goal is to be right more often than you're wrong, and not to fall in love with a wrong idea, allowing your mistakes to get costly.

The single product on which I probably made the most money was a wristwatch calendar I initially had rejected. The item was a small aluminum band with a monthly calendar printed on it. It had four tabs, which would bend around your watchstrap to attach the calendar. This was in 1965, before digitals.

When it was first presented to me, I scoffed. "Who's going to put this cheap piece of aluminum on a good watch? Would you put it on your Rolex? That's an expensive piece of jewelry!"

The manufacturer's representative was a friend who lived in Phoenix. "Look," he said patiently, "everyone wants to know the time, and they want to know the date. Here you have a calendar right on your wristwatch, where you always need it. It's really a good product, and we're starting to have some success with it."

I didn't agree.

"Just give it a shot," he said. "Show it at one of your sales meetings."

I said I'd do it, as a favor. The next sales meeting came up. I was presenting what I considered a very hot product, and it wasn't the wristband calendar. I must have spent 20 minutes pitching, elaborating, and firing up the sales force on this new product. Today, I don't remember what that product was.

Finally, I held up the little wristband calendar and I said to my salesmen, "Look, this is a little product that Sherwin Block has, and he's a good friend, and I don't know . . . see if you can sell it, okay?"

The next day I had ten orders. And volume just kept building each day with more and more orders. I did a double take. I couldn't believe it, but it really was a hot item. In a lifetime of selling, you very seldom come up with a product this hot.

We sold the calendars for about $1 for a set of 12, after paying the supplier 60¢. He charged the same price, whether you bought 100 or 1,000. The aluminum calendars were packed in a small clear-plastic case and a card was inserted that said, "Compliments of ——." The blank was filled in with the name, address, and phone number of the company that was giving them away.

After a couple of months of escalating volume, one of my salesmen said, "Jack, I've got a hell of a deal here. A pharmaceutical company wants to buy sixty thousand sets of wristband calendars." Now that was a big order. I congratulated him.

"Except," he added, "they want to put the names of four pharmaceutical products on the tabs that fold under the watchband. And they want a better deal on the price."

I computed the figures. The client wanted 60,000 sets of 12—that was 720,000 pieces. For an order that large, he deserved a better price.

"No problem," I said. "That should be easy enough to arrange." I called the manufacturer. "We have a deal for sixty thousand sets of calendars. They want some imprinting on the tabs and a better break on the price," I said.

"The price is the same, and we don't imprint the calendars," the man said.

"Wait a minute," I said. "You print the months on the calendars. Isn't that printing?"

"Yeah," he said.

"Well, why don't you just print on the prongs at the same time," I suggested. "The added cost is nothing."

"No extras," he said flatly. "We only do it this way. And the price is sixty cents a set, no matter how many you buy."

I couldn't believe it. Here was man with the opportunity to take a larger order than he had ever received, and he was not only inflexible but surly.

I called Jerry, our production man. "Take a look at this," I said. "See what it takes to make them because I'm doing business with an idiot."

Jerry returned the next day and said, "It's easy. The tooling is relatively inexpensive. We can manufacture them for about thirty cents a set."

We took the order from the pharmaceutical company, made the calendars ourselves, and sold them the 60,000 sets for 66¢ a set. A few months later my friend called me from Phoenix. "Jack, I've got a real problem," he said. "I've got customers all over the country who are on programs with watchband calendars. I can't sell them. My manufacturer is folding."

I wasn't surprised. The man went bankrupt for several reasons. First, he didn't understand dated items. If you have a million items that say "January 1965" in February you might as well burn them. Second, you don't remain inflexible in the pricing of large orders. It was a mentality similar to the man who asserted he didn't make portfolios.

My friend asked if I could supply the calendars to his distributors around the country. "Sure," I said, and we entered the business of supplying all the other distributors of watchband calendars. In our second year we sold 23 million watchband calendars. And that's a product I thought would never sell.

The moral, of course, is that in spite of experience with this kind of merchandise, I still guessed wrong. Don't maintain a position when you are wrong, whether buying or selling. Acknowledge the truth and stay flexible.

Products—and How to Qualify Them

I classify merchandise into three categories: standard, hot, and trademark. A standard item is something that is going to be, or has been, traded for years and years—a steady seller. It will never be a huge winner or loser. It is generally nonexclusive, yet still profitable over the long haul. It's a good product.

The "hot" item is unpatentable, you can't copyright it, and you know you are going to get monstrous competition as soon as people hear about it. You have to get in fast, hit hard, and get the hell out. This takes exquisite timing. You don't want to be stuck with the last shipment of Davy Crockett hats or pet rocks when the fads have run their course.

The final category is the product you develop as an exclusive identifying trademark line; a brand name that you own. This is the most permanent product, and the business to go after.

The establishment of a brand image is worth more than most other assets. If you just put out no-namers, they may be great, but each item has to stand on its own. On the other hand, people buy a brand as long as it continues to supply good style and fine quality. They buy the line because of its reputation.

The ideal, of course, is to become the generic name in the business. That's the ultimate in brand identification. For years, people didn't buy refrigerators; they bought Frigidaires. Even now, they don't buy a cola drink if they can buy a Coke.

This generic recognition is difficult to attain, and it often takes years. Dropping down a notch, it is not quite as difficult to create an exclusive trademark line, a proprietary item. We did it in 1980, with the licensing of the Pierre Cardin line. Once again, it was a deal that happened through necessity.

I received a call from the Sheaffer Pen Company and immediately told the bad news to Albert Lucky, my associate in Europe. "Jim Thomas of Sheaffer just told me they are not going to extend our contract, which expires in six months." I could feel the dismay and shock at the other end of the line. It matched mine.

"But this is impossible!" he said finally. "It will ruin us!"

"It's not going to ruin us," I consoled, "but it sure is going to give us a hell of a blow."

In the specialty advertising business, the closest thing to a staple is the pen, and being exclusive distributor of a brand-name pen of good quality at a moderate price made you a winner. I knew we had done a fantastic job for Sheaffer. We had shown them a market in Europe for their low-priced plastic pens. They had been thrilled with the results.

I suspected that, at the insistence of their managers in the United Kingdom, they decided they could do the same distribution we were doing, without using us as the exclusive distributor. Nothing was further from the truth, however. They did not have the talent, the knowledge, or the ability to do that specialized job. But that didn't make our situation any easier. We were sitting with a large assembly plant, sensational distribution throughout the European Common Market countries, and no product. We were out in the cold.

I returned to France the following month to see what could be done about replacing the volume provided by the Sheaffer line. I became very aware of how tired I was of developing streams of business for various manufacturers without controlling any proprietary items. In 1980, however, it was going to be very difficult, without spending enormous amounts of money, to manufacture a writing instrument that could become a brand name overnight.

It was a warm, restless night and my thoughts weren't leading me anywhere. I went for a walk. I took off my suit, shirt, and tie and reached for a pair of jeans and T-shirt. As I lifted the jeans I noticed the name Pierre Cardin on the back pocket. And inspiration struck. If designer names could sell jeans and other clothing, perfumes, and many other products, why not writing instruments? A designer name would give immediate identification and probably a more desirable product. I decided to obtain a license from an international designer to manufacture his line of writing instruments—a line I could own and control.

I met with Albert Lucky at our factory in Grasse, France, and told him what I had in mind. At first he was sceptical, but he warmed to the idea when I explained the rationale. We chose three names and would call on them in that order. First came the best-known name in the world—Pierre Cardin—followed by Yves St. Laurent and Christian Dior.

That day, Albert called Pierre Cardin's headquarters in Paris and talked to the person second-in-command. The next day we flew to Paris and began a whirlwind series of negotiations to manufacture and sell a line of writing instruments designed by Cardin.

After six months of discussions and examinations of the designer's demands, we approached agreement and contracts reached draft stage. When we received our contract draft, unfortunately it mentioned that no other name could appear on the same product with Pierre Cardin's.

This was impossible, of course. Our total distribution was in advertising specialties that featured the advertiser's name imprinted on each pen. Pierre Cardin's name would appear on the clip of the pen as the brand name, and the name of the bank, insurance company, or manufacturer would appear on the barrel. The gentleman in charge of licensing such product lines insisted that no other name appear with Cardin's. I explained that it was absolutely essential that we have the right to put an advertiser's name on the barrel.

He was shocked. "Do you mean that you want to put the name of a butcher beside Pierre Cardin's?" he asked, aghast at the impropriety of it all. It was obvious that further discussions would be futile. I asked for a meeting with Mr. Cardin.

Fortunately, Mr. Cardin was in the building and we got an audience. And fortunately also, Mr. Cardin was an astute businessman. I explained the principles of what we did, and our subsequent predicament. He looked at me for a moment and said, "How many will you sell this way?"

"Millions," I replied.

"Okay," he said, and the deal was made.

Pierre Cardin designed a magnificent writing instrument for us—one that looked unlike any other pen on the market. From the very beginning, it had a unique appeal. We had the first models made in six months and, a year later, produced our first line. It was introduced to our distributors in Europe at L'Espace Pierre Cardin in Paris. The pen was an instant hit and we did, indeed, sell millions. We still do.

Through licensing of a famous name and by having one of the world's top designers actually design the product line, we were able to produce a proprietary line of products. This has since expanded into office equipment, stationery, paper goods, and other related products. We had a well-known brand name from day one, giving us immediate entry into the marketplace.

Licensing is a tremendous concept, one we have expanded on successfully since that first encounter. In our European operation today, Pierre Cardin products are responsible for 75 percent of our business. It is our own brand name—one we completely control. The seemingly devastating blow from Sheaffer put us on our toes and made us come up with an optimum solution. It resulted in far better business than we had before.

I admit that it's not easy to tie up licensing rights on a product. Much of our success came as a result of the reputation we had created in the field. Time is a major factor, however. Currently, we are developing a new line of designer writing instruments. The time from concept and sketches, through hand model, on to production and marketing can span 18 to 24 months. An entrepreneur beginning a career or trying to make a name for himself doesn't have the luxury of time. The next best (and easier) thing to do is to go to Milan, Frankfurt, or Tokyo and find something you really like. Obtain exclusive distribution rights to the product, then go out and sell it. But this path is not without its pitfalls either.

To Buy or Not to Buy

Trade shows are heady experiences. The temptations to buy are sometimes irresistible. You attend a trade show to find a product you can sell in the United States. With this purpose shaping your thinking, you have to be very, very, careful.

It's easy to be seduced. Once we were at a trade show in Düsseldorf, where a particular item was stealing the limelight. It was a different kind of key holder, called a Klik because it clicked into place. The Klik was being merchandised at the booth with impressive point-of-purchase materials and a lot of glamour. The display attracted all kinds of attention, and the positive action of the gadget drove everyone crazy.

It was interesting, but in the final analysis it was just a key holder. Nevertheless, my partner fell in love with the idea and began negotiating for exclusive United States distribution. This was several years after our Courier key holder, which was very successful for us, and he was looking for another hot item. The Courier, however, was a combination product: both key holder and pen. The Klik was simply a gimmicky key holder.

In the Courier deal, we dealt with a very amenable Italian. But this was different. The company was German, and they thought they had reinvented the wheel. They had a big winner here, they thought, and they didn't want just one order. They wanted a five-year program, with a commitment for large quantities each year at escalating prices. I said there was no way we would do that. My partner and I agreed to make a one-year commitment, only if the deal was in dollars. (The dollar was strong at the time, and I knew what our cost was.) If the dollar weakened and we had bought in deutsch marks, it would increase our actual cost.

The negotiations continued. They insisted on a longer period and that payment be in marks, "because that's what we buy and sell in." When we left Düsseldorf, a representative met us in Milan to continue the talks. I had to leave early, and my partner all but made the deal. I finally vetoed the whole thing.

The bottom line was that it was a *novelty* item, which never lasts past a year. In the first year, it's a new story and everyone loves it; after that, it's an old story and you're sitting with a warehouse full of novelties you can't give away. If there's more utility than novelty to it, the item may evolve into a statement. *May.* But to make a three- to five-year commitment was absolutely out of the question. Ultimately, someone else bought it and took a beating. The Klik was never successful in the United States.

But we *could* have made the deal. Everyone thought this was a great product, and if I had agreed with "everyone," we would have had a catastrophe on our hands. It is very tricky to make a commitment without backing it up with proper research. Yet people do it all the time. Sometimes an item can fool you totally, and you fall right off the mountain. You think you're the greatest merchandiser in the world. You've had a history of successes. Then suddenly you buy a complete dud or turn down a product that is the greatest thing since sliced bread (as I did initially with the wristband calendars). But the difference between the two situations is that the wristband calendar, although a novelty, had a one-of-a-kind utilitarian function; the Klik had a function, too, but so did any number of other key holders.

You want to get the best results with the least risk. It takes us back to whether your company is going to be market driven or product driven. If you act hastily and place a large order for something, you have to sell it. And it may turn out to be an item not too easy to sell. Anyone can sell a good product, but no one—no matter how good a salesman—can sell a bad product for any length of time. A product usually is either good or bad—rarely in between. The market tells you which is which.

We are very diligent about setting overall goals for our business, because a business can get sucked into almost anything, particularly in international trade. Once you're in the marketplace, the deals keep coming. You have to distinguish between what fits and what doesn't. Just because it's a good deal doesn't mean it's a good deal for you. If I wear size 44 long jacket and a guy offers me a 38 long, I can't wear it. It doesn't fit. It could be the finest material available and the biggest bargain, but it doesn't do me any good. It's the same in business. The product, the finances, the distribution, the overall game plan—all have to fit. If they don't the deal won't work.

Research

A businessman can spend a lot of money on market research. Usually, the research offers some variation on the question, "If I had this product, would you buy it?" I won't spend a dime on that kind of research. It's worthless.

For an entrepreneur, primary market research involves going to a customer and saying, "I have this product, and I'd like to sell it to you. Will you buy it?" You'll get an accurate answer right away. It's true that there are sophisticated, accurate forms of market research. But for someone with limited means, who has to find out right away if he has a salable item, the best research is to try to sell it—before making a commitment.

If you return from a trade fair and hand samples of a product to your salesmen, with instructions to hit the field, you'll soon know whether you have a dog or a winner. If they come back saying, "Boy, that's a dog. Nobody wants it," then you're out only a little time and energy. But if they come back and say, "Yeah, we made thirty calls and got ten orders; this is a piece of cake," you can make your commitment. You've done your market research, and now you know you can safely place a big order.

The main problem with this approach is that by taking just samples you generally can't tie up an exclusive. I don't recommend this to most people, but if you're a craggy old veteran like me and really know your business, you can do what I did with the Courier key holder. When I first saw the Courier at a trade fair, years of experience told me it was a winner and that I had to tie it up, then and there. I put money on the line and made my commitment immediately. Obviously, my chances of making large profits were greater. And my chances of losing were much greater, too. Risk and profit are directly proportionate, as always.

But even craggy old veterans can get fooled. You have to qualify your product, as best you can under whatever restrictions you operate. There are many questions you have to ask yourself: Do you have prior knowledge of the product? Is it the first time you've ever seen the product? Just because it's new doesn't make it good. Like the Klik, the product could be new and lousy. What is the *real* potential?

If you've located a potential item, your next step is to compute your costs. This is an area of risk for novices. Suppose the manufacturer will sell it to you for 10¢ a piece. What does it cost to have that product sitting in your warehouse? A veteran would know his costs within a point or two, for instance, based on duty of 20 percent, freight charges of 10 percent, brokerage fees of another 5 percent, insurance of such and such, handling of so much, and an extra allowance for pricing it too low. A novice has to do it the hard way. You have to go through each step, from the product's weight onwards.

After doing all this, if you discover that the product costs you 15¢ by the time it reaches your warehouse, you then find out what similar products are selling for in the United States and where the best distribution would be (see Chapter 9). By the time you total all these factors, you have qualified your product. Your next step is either to pre-sell samples as a test or, if that isn't possible, to place a relatively small order so you can test the waters. Order 10,000 items, go only $1,500 into the hole, then take it out and peddle it. If the product is successful, you are now in a position to crystallize your costs and your profits. Go back to the manufacturer who quoted 10¢ a piece and ask for a quote on a million pieces.

On the other hand, if after two months you find you have 9,000 pieces left, close them out, dump them, and go on to the next thing—a little wiser and not much poorer. Remember the principle: you can't promote a dog. A dog is a dog, and a great item is a great item.

Remember what I said earlier about going with your strengths and dropping your weaknesses. It's easier said than done, of course. Almost any company does 80 percent of its business with 20 percent of its products. It's simple to say, "Drop the other 80 percent," but you don't always know what they are. There's the famous story of the newcomer in the advertising department of Wrigley Chewing Gum, who said, "Mr. Wrigley, I want you to know that you're wasting 50 percent of your advertising money." Wrigley's response was, "If you tell me which 50 percent of it is, I'll be glad to drop it."

Qualifying your products is an ongoing process. You get better at it as time goes by. Generally, however, you don't have much time in the beginning stages. Speed is more essential today than ever before. Even our domestic food companies have changed the way they do business. They used to put out a product in a test city to see the reaction. Fewer are doing that these days. The American marketplace is so hungry for new products that the minute they test-market all the competitors have samples, which they analyze. By the time the original product goes to market, the competitors have put together copies. If the item is successful, they have five imitators. The same applies on a smaller scale to international marketing. If you find a product, it's best to be there first with the most. If you can hedge your bet with pre-selling, your chances for success are excellent.

How to Work a Trade Show

Trade shows are probably the best way to enter a market—or find it. Here, in one place, you can find products to buy, sell products you manufacture or represent, and see what the competition is up to. But trade shows also can be a distraction and a tremendous waste of time and energy if you don't know how to work them properly.

Know your purpose for being at the trade show. If you're a manufacturer, you're there to sell; if you're a buyer, you're there to buy. Peripheral benefits include building an industry image, maintaining contact with current customers, assessing the competition, and so forth, but to maximize your investment, keep your primary purpose in the forefront.

As an Exhibitor

It's sometimes difficult to sustain your purpose amid the roar of the crowd and the smell of the greasepaint. Let's look first at the problems you encounter as an exhibitor and consider how best to handle them.

Time is one of your costliest and most valuable assets, and you don't want to waste it. Many people don't understand that they've paid for the time to be at a trade show. You've only got so much time—one day or three days—to tell your story to so many people.

To maximize your time, qualify your customers and make sure your booth people know how to qualify. Be able to tell the difference between a live prospect and a dead one. The duds are the people who take all your time, while your best potential accounts are standing on the fringes, trying to get an audience—until they move on to someone else's booth.

There are only two ways to qualify customers: to observe and to ask. If you don't know your buyers by sight, watch those badges. If you're selling microchips and a guy comes by with an I.B.M. badge, drop everything to talk to him. Keep your eyes open. The person who can really do the job for you may be trying to fight his way through the crowd of lookers.

If I'm at an international trade show and a distributor I don't know comes over, how do I qualify him? I ask very politely about his operation. "May I ask, sir, what your distribution is? How many pens do you buy a year? What is your budget?" It's as simple as that. I don't waste time asking how his golf game is or what he thinks of the weather in Germany. I keep it strictly business.

At an electronics show recently I saw a huge booth where *Playboy* centerfold models were autographing copies of the magazine. It wasn't a *Playboy* booth; it belonged to a radio manufacturer. But the traffic at the booth was great. It was filled with bored men who wanted to look at girls. The company wasn't selling any radios. At many shows you'll find booths with comedians, magicians, girls in swimsuits, or just about anything else that can be dreamed up. It's a complete waste.

When I put a booth together I leave off the bells and whistles. I simply find the most attractive way to display my merchandise and tell my story. I don't want models or magicians or anything else that is going to distract from what I have to sell. There are more effective ways to attract people to the booth. I would rather create a pre-exhibit direct mail program, sent to the people I want to see at the convention, offering them a premium or specialty as an incentive to get them to come by. When they come to the booth as a result of that premium, I don't want anything to distract them from my merchandise. When exhibiting at a trade show, everything I do is designed to sell my products or my process. I want serious buyers to visit me. If we establish a social relationship, I may take the prospect to dinner, but I'm not going to indulge in distractions during the show.

Do your homework before the show. Target your customers and invest in a mailing or series of mailings that will get them to your booth. If you can induce them to come to you first, you've half-sold your product. The rest gets easier.

The next, terribly important rule is to break your neck to get the best possible space. A friend of mine sells women's hosiery. He complained to me once about how he arrived at a womenswear show to find his booth in the sportswear area. I didn't give him much sympathy. Why didn't he know where his booth was before the show started?

When I go to a trade show, the first thing I do is find the spot where I'll get the most traffic. My second question is, "Who's next to me?" I don't want a magician there, distracting *my* audience. On the other hand, I *do* want to be beside a really strong noncompetitive company that attracts a lot of people. I don't want competitors near me because I don't want them to see what I'm doing. Do what it takes to get the best booth possible. It's worth the effort.

Another necessity is to have your booth manned by the right people. Certain people are excellent at trade shows or conventions, and others are not. Some people are great on long-range selling and bad on short-range closing. If it's a hard-sell show and you are there because you have a product you want to really move, man the booth with hard-sell closing people who always say, "How many?" early in the conversation. If it is not a selling show, have your booth manned by the rep who regularly calls in that territory.

These are some of the basic rules of exhibiting. Get the right booth, have the right people to command that booth, do the right promotion before the show to get the customers to the booth, qualify the people who visit the booth to sort out the buyers, and don't distract the customers. Get your story across fast, and get the order. It's a winning formula.

As a Buyer

If you are a buyer attending a trade show, there are ways you can maximize your time and investment. For instance, keep your purpose for being there paramount and don't get distracted. You are there for two or three days, and in that time you have to see as much as you possibly can, because you're probably not coming back for another year. I try to get a floor plan before the show begins, then determine by location the fastest way to travel up and down the aisles without missing anything. Your purpose is to assess the show and its offering.

Often you will find that the smallest booths offer the greatest gems. The biggest booth generally is controlled by the biggest company. That big company usually has nothing new to show and won't do business with you anyway, since it already has its distribution. The smaller guy is often the fellow who has gotten into the show for the first time and has a hot new product. It's where you find the real winning items.

Spot the products that are of most interest, but travel the whole show. Look at everything. Many people go to shows and visit only the people they know, saying they don't have time to see anything new. That's ridiculous. What are they doing there? Take the time to look at the guy who isn't well established, because you'll find he's the guy you can do more business with.

Follow your plan to traverse the show and do a fast go-around. I travel down the aisles at a pace that's slow enough for me to see almost everything but fast enough to resist the temptation to stop anywhere. If I see something interesting, I note it in the pad I carry. After I've done this, I have the general feel of the show, I know how many exhibitors are selling relatively the same products, and which products I am interested in.

My second pass through the show is to see people I might have made appointments with earlier or others I've been doing business with or those who's product line I really want to see for some reason. On my third pass I visit the booths I marked down from the first time around.

How do you approach a booth? It varies according to who you are, of course. I'm very miserly about my time, particularly at a trade show, so I try to get the most done in the shortest time. Nowadays, because my business is well established, I'm a big buyer. Because of my distribution, I'm going to purchase large quantities. I want the special attention that's given to big buyers, not for my ego, but because I want the best price, the best consideration, and the possibility of an exclusive relationship.

Suppose I want to go back to a booth where I saw something I really liked. I know I'm a big buyer, but the man in the booth doesn't know that. Nor do I know who the boss is. If I'm a big buyer, I want to talk to the head man—the person I can make a deal with. Instead of hitting him head on, I carry some personal publicity with me—perhaps my brochure or something else that shows I'm a big buyer. Then I go to this very busy booth and politely ask whoever is free to take a moment with me. I introduce myself and my company, and I tell him we have world distribution. I hand him my brochure and whatever other articles I brought, and I ask for a specific appointment with the principal to discuss my business. When I come back, the head guy has read my material, knows who I am, and is ready to meet with me. I have set the proper atmosphere to make my time in that booth as productive as possible.

I often tell the people who work with me, "Use all the muscle the company has." If you don't have that muscle, if you have little experience, no offices around the world, no distribution to speak of, and only some bright ideas, you use whatever you have—your intellect, your capability. If that is your situation, stay away from the big, established companies and look for a hot new product carried by a smaller and newer manufacturer. Still try to see the head man. It may take a little longer, but he is there to sell, and if you appear competent, he'll be willing to discuss the possibilities with you. You may walk away with samples or an agreement to do business.

Maximizing the Trade Show

Trade shows are a terrific place for an American manufacturer who wants to test the export waters. If you have a product that has been successful in the United States, have production capabilities you can expand, and know that your costs will go down if you can find more distribution, go to a trade show on a fact-finding expedition to see what the market is. Find out what products are directly competitive with yours. Then start talking to a few people about your product. Bring plenty of literature with you. Also make sure you either bring someone with you who really knows the language or arrange for a translator to travel with you. All major conventions have translators for hire at rates that range from $10 to $20 an hour. The $75 or so a day is a smart investment.

At an international show almost every booth has someone who speaks English, but there are some that don't. Even among those that do, however, you often find that the person speaks only "surface" English, which is not good enough when you get into the details of business or try to make a deal. Not only will your communications be more accurate with a translator, but I guarantee that you'll see an expression of relief on the seller's face. He's tremendously happy that he doesn't have to speak English anymore, and you're following the prime rule of business: making it easy for the other guy to do business with you.

Trade shows can be very effective, whether you buy or sell. Follow these basic rules and you will ensure that your time and money are spent in the most productive manner.

Gut Feelings

They call it gut feeling, intuition, instinct. Although never defined very well or even understood very often, gut feeling is an important element of every businessman's life. I have a great respect for gut feelings; they are instincts that have been developed by performing. What I think of as intuition may be reality tempered by experience.

There's a saying, "The harder I work, the luckier I get." The more you work and the more you pump into yourself, the truer your instincts become. They are created by a series of successes and failures, filtered through experience. What comes out is pure. I've learned to trust my instincts. When I have gone against them and rationalized a deal, it has never worked out.

In 1976, when M.M.S. International was exhibiting at its first trade show in Düsseldorf, one of the problems we faced was distribution. I had several long conversations on the subject with our managing director, Albert Lucky. He told me he wanted to appoint an exclusive distributor in Germany. All the other distributors could buy from him. "I've had success with this way of distribution," Lucky said, adding, "This man knows everyone in Germany, and he's very friendly with the other distributors."

My gut feelings told me it was basically wrong. All my experience said that people don't buy from their competitors. I told Albert my misgivings.

"Maybe that's the case in the United States, but it's different in Europe," he said. "It's particularly different in Germany. You need an exclusive distributor there." In spite of my gut telling me no, I went along with it, figuring that Albert (who was European and had done business there for many years) knew more about the European market than I did.

It was a disaster. Our German distributor never sold the merchandise to his competitors. The arrangement lasted only one season, but it destroyed us in Germany for several years. A number of German distributors told me "How can we buy from him? He's our competitor." Bad news travels fast, while good news takes a longer route. It took a long time to get the word out to other distributors that they could buy from us directly. My gut feeling was right; the advice was bad. I went along with it, and I regretted it.

Lucky's experience had been with bulk merchandise, in which distributors in certain companies ordered massive numbers of pens and distributed them to every kind of trade. The specialty advertising business is different: intensely competitive and a much narrower field involving far smaller orders. He went by his experience, which didn't apply in this case; and I ignored mine, which did. Big mistake.

Intuitive responses are usually immediate, and aren't something you have to think about. Listen to them and trust them, because instincts have information not readily available to the intellect. More often than not, snap judgments are really responses based on your experiences. Just be sure that your instincts aren't conning yourself because you want them that way for some reason.

This is true of products and of deals, but nowhere is it truer than in your choice of people with whom you do business. People can have the greatest credentials in the world, but if your instincts warn you against them, trust your instincts. Instincts are, perhaps, a businessman's most valuable asset.

6

The Art of
Negotiation

Excellence in negotiating is something we all aspire to. And negotiation is something we have all done for as long as we can remember. As children we negotiated for a later bedtime or for dessert before dinner, as teenagers we negotiated for dad's car, as employees we negotiated for a raise. As businessmen or women we negotiate a deal. We are always negotiating, though much of the time we are not aware of it.

The methods and nuances of negotiation are as varied as people. There are whiners—those who seek sympathy by saying, "Give me a break. I'm a good guy. Give me the deal rather than anyone else." There are blusterers—bluffers—who threaten to get their own way and who bludgeon you into a deal. There are the "spit and polish" guys who use their suede-shoe routines to dazzle you.

There's the famous negotiating story about the guy who asks the girl he just met if she'll go to bed with him for a million dollars.

"Sure," she says. "That's ridiculous. Of course I'd go to bed with you for a million bucks."

"Will you go to bed with me for $10?" he asks.

"What do you think I am?" she asks indignantly.

"We've already established what you are," he says. "We're just negotiating price now."

Negotiations position you and the other party, although not necessarily in adversarial roles. Negotiation should clarify and simplify, rather than complicate, the deal. If conducted properly, negotiation is the oil that greases the wheels of a deal, making it workable, efficient, and an arrangement in which everyone gets what he wants.

Dozens of books have been written about negotiation, many with which I disagree. I don't believe in negotiating through intimidation, fear, bluffing, or dishonest tactics. A good negotiation concludes as a good deal for everyone.

My negotiations have always been based on the reality of the deal. Everything goes back to the deal—the basic, basic deal. What is my position? What is the position of the other party? What do we both want? Most people think of business negotiations in terms of price, but many other factors are involved. Along with price you negotiate materials, quality, quantity, delivery times, financing, contract length, participation, and as many other subjects as necessary. But it's all grounded in the essence of the deal.

Negotiating can be very subtle. It can range from the simplest terms—how much and how many—to vast complexities. However, even the complexities should be broken down into their basic parts. When a negotiation gets too complex, the deal can be lost in complexities. Once the deal is lost, everyone has lost.

Negotiation starts with what you want to accomplish. Then the realities and, sometimes, the complexities enter the picture. Sometimes many points of view and many elements have to be considered, but the deal itself must always be kept in view.

Negotiating Successes

Let me tell you about a couple of deals I made, and the negotiations that went into creating them. Although only one applies particularly to international trade, they were both in their way landmark deals in my business career and they will illustrate a number of valuable points.

Selling and Buying Back the Business

It was the fall of 1968. We had spent 15 years building a solid business, taking it from zero to $4 million in sales, with offices in Los Angeles and San Francisco and some 15 salespeople. We were the leading specialty advertising company on the West Coast, with an excellent reputation.

The operation was simple—pretty much seat-of-the-pants. We were not involved in sophisticated projections or budgets or extensive long-range planning. We knew above all that we had to buy for one price and sell for another; that we had to keep a strong, lean operation; and that we had to make a profit. We did it well.

It was also the age of conglomeration, however, and Jack Nadel, Inc., was about to get caught in the acquisition net. One Thursday morning, my salesman Joe Seinfeld called to say he had a client who would like to meet me. The man's name was Don Gevirtz, and he worked for Republic Corporation, a large conglomerate.

The meeting puzzled me at first. Don immediately started to ask questions about my business rather than about merchandise to buy, which is why I thought he was there. With him was a fellow named Gene Duchene, president of the Krupp Organization, a recently acquired direct-mail division of Republic. He rode shotgun while Don asked all the questions. I had the feeling I was talking to student and teacher.

As we got further into the meeting, it was revealed that Don was in charge of Republic's acquisitions. He had heard about Jack Nadel, Inc., and asked if I'd be interested in selling the business. I said I'd certainly listen to whatever proposition they had.

I realized they were quite serious, even though they had no idea what the specialty business was all about. Unfortunately, I didn't realize until much later that the same was probably true with regard to the machine-tool business, the aircraft business, the oil business, the steel business, the paper business, the printing business, the direct-mail business, the agency business, and the many other types of companies Republic had acquired.

Republic Corporation, formerly the Republic Pictures that had made film stars of John Wayne, Roy Rogers, Gene Autry, Monty Hale and others in the thirties and forties, had been taken over in 1966 by an entrepreneur named Gerald Block. At that time the total market value of the company was $10 million—2.5 million shares at $4 per share. Block sold the film library and some real estate for about $12 million and went on an acquisitions binge with the cash, acquiring some 80 different companies in two years. Only the first two acquisitions were for cash. After those the stock rose in value and subsequent companies were bought on a tax-free exchange of stock. Republic Corporation was listed on the New York Stock Exchange, doing some $400 million in business and selling for about 40 times its earnings. In those days, conglomerates were the golden-haired darlings of Wall Street.

We entered an intense negotiating period. The usual conversations between buyer and seller took place. I would say, "Well, I wasn't really thinking of selling. I'm perfectly happy the way I am."

And the buyer would say, "Well, there are so many things you can do that you can't do now if you're part of our company."

Later, with the wisdom of hindsight, I compared it to the kid who sits on the corner with a sign that says, "Dog For Sale." The mutt is sitting beside him, and a guy walks up and says, "Johnny, how much do you want for that dog?"

"$50,000," he says.

The guy laughs, pats him on the head, and leaves. Two days later, he comes back to find the sign and the dog gone. "What happened?" he asks the kid.

"I sold my dog," Johnny says.

"Did you get your price?"

"Sure did."

"You mean you got $50,000?"

"Not exactly," Johnny says. "I got two $25,000 cats."

Our deal was made in three weeks. After 15 years of building Jack Nadel, Inc., we sold to Republic Corporation for 50,000 shares of Republic stock valued at $2 million.

It was a tax-free exchange of stock—our privately held stock in exchange for stock in a publicly held corporation—giving us a net worth we had never before determined. There was a catch, however. It was restricted stock, which meant it couldn't be sold for at least three years. An incentive clause said that if we met certain requirements, we could earn an additional 50,000 shares, which would give us a net value of $4 million. It was fair. I was willing to risk a drop in the stock price because I felt the upside had the same potential as the down.

I learned about greed. Within a year, our original 50,000 shares, which were initially worth $40, had risen to $90 a share. Our $2 million was now worth $4.5 million. If we continued to do excellent business, it looked very much as if we would double our stock interest over the three-year period and end up with $9 million. My head spun with grandiose dreams.

All this changed a year later, when the market reversed itself and the stock started to drop. People who had sold their companies, exchanging years of effort for Republic stock, saw their fortunes collapse further each day. To make matters worse, suddenly every division of the conglomerate—almost without exception—was losing money. It was like watching a giant whale get all the air taken out of it and shrink in size, power, and capability.

Republic had created a house of cards—or a fairytale. They called it the story of synergism. *Synergy* was a buzzword of the sixties. What it purported to be was the ability of one division or entity within a corporation to relate to another. In other words, if one made something and the other sold something, it was in the same basic line of business and they added to each other's potential. So it was not just earnings investors were buying, it was synergism! For a while, analysts fell for the fairy tale.

It didn't take me long to figure out that this was a meaningless word. It was used to rationalize almost anything that was done, and somehow conglomerates had been able to convince stock market analysts that there was a synergy—or real relationship—among a machine shop, a coal mine, and an advertising specialty company.

Quite apart from what was happening to the stock, Republic was a very uncomfortable experience. I was out of the arena of people who did business and now in the arena of people who juggled numbers. These numbers people did not create anything; they just moved the figures around and swept the problems under the carpet. I felt that business had an obligation to produce, to offer opportunities for its employees and to create a profit for its stockholders.

I'll never forget one incident that happened in the midst of all the chaos and disaster. Of the 80 divisions, 75 were losing money. Jack Nadel, Inc., continued to increase its volume and make more profit. One month, I happily reported that projections for that period almost doubled because of a large deal we had no way of anticipating. It's the kind of thing that can happen in the specialty business, and we were, of course, delighted. But our group vice president called. "Jack," he said irritably. "I gotta tell you something. You guys can't project worth a damn!"

"I beg your pardon," I said. "I don't quite understand."

"Well," he said, "you made twice as much profit as you projected, and I don't know how we can plan for this."

For a second I was stunned, and then I responded. "I think you are a total ass," I said. "Seventy-five divisions are losing money, the company is struggling on the brink of disaster, and you've got one little gold mine pumping better than expected. And you take the time to chastise me for not projecting properly? I think I'm going home to read *Alice in Wonderland!*" I made up my mind to buy back Jack Nadel, Inc., but this wouldn't happen for several more years—the most challenging, emotionally wrenching years of my career.

In June 1970, Gerald Block called me into his office and told me with great logic that the stock was falling. The public just didn't recognize the true value of Republic, because there were so many divisions and different businesses. The parts, he said, were really worth more than the whole. He wanted to take a group of companies and float a separate public issue. For the first time, I received a compliment. Block told me I had the best-run company in the group. He wanted me to start a subsidiary of Republic and float a separate public issue to provide financing for the parent corporation and set patterns for deals to come. He offered me the job as president and chief executive officer of the new subsidiary, made up of all the advertising and marketing divisions. It would eventually become Measured Marketing Services, Inc.

I agreed, on the condition that I be given the ability to sell some of my Republic stock to gain my own liquidity. It took some strong negotiating, but they finally agreed to clear 25 percent of my stock for immediate sale and another 25 percent six months later. At this point the stock was $25 a share, and dropping.

The first six months in my new job consisted of a great deal of hard work examining the various operations, determining their viability, and deciding whether to keep or dispose of them. In the meantime, my attempts to get my stock cleared were being subverted. Somehow, the legal department of Republic could never quite get around to doing the rather simple task of clearing the first 25 percent of my stock for sale. The value of the stock was still dropping, and I was watching my personal fortune vanish.

My attorney at the time was quite capable, but he was terribly polite and afforded the attorneys at Republic "professional courtesy." There was a lot of nice conversation, but my stock wasn't getting cleared. I decided to find out if any lettered stock had ever been cleared at Republic. It was a cloak-and-dagger operation. From a contact in the legal department secretarial pool, I discovered that the fellow who had originally acquired Jack Nadel, Inc., for Republic had had his stock cleared for sale. I checked further and found out he was no longer with the company. Still more checking turned up his attorney's name, Howard Sterling.

Sterling was a young man of medium height and slender build, with bushy hair and large glasses. He was brilliant and tough. I told him my problem and asked if he could get the stock cleared. He said he could if allowed to get tough. I agreed, and asked how much he got paid. At that time his fee was $100 an hour, which was very high. I didn't want to pay $100 an hour and be left holding the sack, so he agreed to charge me a flat fee of $10,000 for clearing the stock or a lesser figure for his time if he didn't succeed. We had a deal.

We met with the attorney who headed Republic's legal staff. I stated my case again, and he looked very sympathetic.

"Jack, you know we'd like to get this done right away," he said earnestly, "but we have so many problems right now. It's just going to have to wait its turn." He discussed all the problems Republic had. Howard sat there without opening his mouth.

Finally, when the talk was done, Howard stood up and looked down at the other attorney. "Counselor," he said firmly, "it's very simple. Write down the price of Republic stock today. Then note the price when my client, Jack Nadel, has his stock cleared. And rest assured that I'm going to sue you for the difference and much more if he doesn't get his stock cleared right now."

"But that's not professional courtesy!" the other attorney spluttered in amazement.

"My interest is not to be courteous," Howard said. "You've been screwing around with my client long enough. He has a contract, and his stock should be cleared immediately."

And that's precisely what happened. The $10,000 fee for the little work he did was a bargain. As a matter of fact, I figured out that if I had contacted him three months earlier, I would have been $500,000 richer.

The next few months brought many changes. Gerald Block was deposed and a man named Sanford Sigoloff took his place. Then the plans to float the new Measured Marketing Services issue were shelved when the bottom fell out of the stock market. A couple of abortive attempts were made to sell Measured Marketing Services. Finally, around the time I had almost decided to resign in disgust, Sigoloff was moved over to president and replaced by Roderick Hills, an astute businessman who became chairman of the board. Some years later, Rod Hills served as chairman of the Securities and Exchange Commission.

Through all of this, our subsidiary remained one of the few within the Republic system to show a profit. When I sold to Republic, I had signed a covenant not to compete for five years. That had expired a few months before, and I agonized over whether to leave my own company.

Finally, I had a desperation meeting with my attorney, Howard Sterling. We created an entirely new concept. I did not know it then, but we actually conceived a leveraged buyout—unheard of at that time.

I met with Rod Hills and came directly to the point. "A deal must be made or I'm gone," I said. "If you and I don't come to an agreement by the end of this meeting, I'll resign. I want to be up front with you. I have to make a living, so I'm going to build a new company and take as many people as I can with me."

Rod's face turned white, but he said nothing. I had stated the problem, now it was time to propose a solution. "Let's make a deal," I said. "How much do you want for Measured Marketing Services?"

"Six million dollars," he snapped.

"Okay," I said. "You've got a deal."

He was astounded. "Where are you going to get that kind of money?"

"Now let's talk about the second part of the deal," I said.

When this conversation took place in 1972, Measured Marketing Services was a totally owned subsidiary of Republic Corporation, a failed conglomerate with $40 million in losses and struggling to survive. I began to unfold the plan Howard and I had developed the day before.

I told Rod I wanted to take a 2-year option on Measured Marketing Services to buy the company at $6 million. However, during those two years when Measured Marketing Services was still a subsidiary of Republic, I was to have total control. Instead of sending profits to Republic, I would pay what would normally be paid in corporate income tax. Since I would file a consolidated return, the entire amount would be deductible against Republic's $40 million loss carryforward. So if it earned $1 million that year, I would send up approximately $500,000, representing the tax normally paid on those earnings. And I would deduct the $500,000 from the $6 million I owed Republic. When it was time to exercise the option, I would then pay the net amount out of borrowings.

About 20 months later, that's exactly what happened. I exercised the option and bought the company. By that time, the $6 million had been reduced to $4.2 million, which was borrowed from the Bank of America. Everyone came out a winner. Republic actually got $6 million for the company, and my partners and I took complete control of Measured Marketing Services.

Republic is doing well. Once again they changed management, and as it turned out, Measured Marketing Services was the only company it was able to divest at a figure above its book value. Measured Marketing Services, which my partners and I signed personal guarantees to buy, has since grown into a $100 million company. It was one of the most successful and significant negotiations of my career.

A Merchandise Negotiation

My very first import deal involved an unusual negotiation to ensure the quality of the product we were importing. It was one of the first promotional programs I designed for a supermarket. In 1957, supermarkets were the fastest-growing retail outlets, but it was a competitive environment and they were all anxious to build traffic and create volume.

At the time I was importing cloisonné and cigarette lighters from Japan, and I noticed that a great deal of stainless-steal flatware was being manufactured there very cheaply. Some of it had entered the U.S. market, but it was really junk. You could have cut your tongue on some of the spoons and forks they made.

At the time, we were selling a set of Danish stainless-steel flatware out of our specialty operation. It was beautifully made and gorgeous in appearance, but relatively expensive. I thought that if I could sell something similar in quality that cost a lot less, it would be very successful.

We had an excellent agent in Japan. He really knew the marketplace and all the manufacturers and was extremely reliable. I sent him the Danish set and asked if it could be duplicated in Japan. He said it could.

Vons Markets was an account I was selling to continuously, so I approached the buyer with the set of Danish flatware mounted on a board. I'd prepared a point-of-purchase sign that said, "5-pc. Place Setting—$.99 with any purchase."

"*If*," I asked, "I don't know whether I can, but *if* I could produce this set of five-piece place settings for you to retail at ninety-nine cents, and you could make a 29 percent profit on it, would you be interested?"

"That's impossible," he said.

"Of course," I said. "But I have a quality manufacturer in Japan who can do it."

"I'd give you an order right now if you could guarantee the quality," he said. "But I don't think you'll get it out of the Japanese." In those days, Japan did not have a reputation for quality merchandise.

I told him I'd submit a dozen sample sets and that his order would be subject to approval of those samples. We would guarantee the stock to be as good as the samples. I left the meeting with a provisional order for 100,000 sets, a substantial order in 1957.

My wife, Elly, and I flew to Japan to visit three manufacturers my agent had chosen. We went to the factories, examined their operations, and talked to the principals. After gathering this information, we were able to pick the maker with whom I would negotiate a price.

The negotiation was simple. He asked how many sets I would buy and I said 100,000. My next question was "How much?" and he offered a price.

In Japan at that time and, indeed, anywhere in Asia, you never accepted the first price, no matter how reasonable you thought it was. They would think you an idiot. So I looked at the manufacturer and said one of the three Japanese words I knew, *"Tokai."* Too high.

He entered into a lengthy explanation of how reasonable a price it was. "I surely believe you, and I can understand it," I said (never demean the individual), "but to penetrate our market, we must have a lower price."

I then suggested a price that was less than I expected to pay for it. I'd learned the lesson early never to think that a low price insulted anyone. He grabbed his head and said there was no way he could manufacture it for that cost. We settled somewhere in between. It was a good price, a notch lower than I had been prepared to pay.

Then I did something that was unheard of. I turned to the man I had negotiated with and said, "Now that you have the order, I'm going to ask you to do me a great favor. I want you to turn out flatware of a superb quality."

He replied that their quality was always good, but I shook my head. "No, I mean extra-special quality that's going to take more painstaking manufacturing. More time polishing, more careful examination," I said. And then I added, "I will pay you 10 percent extra if you produce flatware that is comparable to the original Danish set."

He was stunned. No importer had ever voluntarily offered him 10 percent over and above the negotiated price. There was a stipulation, though. I arranged to hire an independent agent who would come into his factory and inspect the merchandise before it was packed to ensure the quality. Furthermore, the letter of credit would call for the inspection certificate, which would be provided by the company I hired.

The quality turned out to be excellent, the maker got his extra 10 percent, and the program was tremendously successful. In four weeks the 100,000 sets sold out in Vons' 26 stores.

Then came an unbelievable tribute to my immaturity and lack of sophistication. The one thing I know now that I didn't know then (at the ripe old age of 33) was that I should have expanded the basic idea. I could have sold this promotion to many major supermarkets in the United States. Instead, I was so thrilled with the results that I ran out and bought a new Cadillac. With the creative juices really flowing, I moved on to another promotion. Today, if I do something successful, you're bound to see it elsewhere, not just around the country, but around the world. I could have become the Flatware King of the World. Instead, I never made or sold another set of flatware.

Both of these deals were important to me, however. The flatware for Vons was one of my first major import deals. Buying back my business from Republic charted an entirely new future for my associates and myself.

When I made the Vons deal I was young, just beginning to develop my negotiating skills. By the time I had to buy my business back, negotiation had become an art, grounded in years of buying and selling, and I had developed some guidelines for the negotiation process.

The Negotiating Art

The very first guideline I try to get across to new salesmen is, "Get away from the other side of the desk." It's also what you have to do in negotiation. Your first step should be to rid yourself of an adversarial position. The reality is that you have a mutual problem, which you are going to solve to your mutual advantage. The intention must be to structure a deal that resolves the problem and gives each of you what you want.

It's not always possible, of course. When it can't be done, you are better off making no deal than making a bad deal. A bad deal usually brings a future filled with enormous problems. Negotiating demands a recognition of reality on many levels.

Only amateurs try to accomplish something that isn't real or possible; it's attempt that inevitably leads to failure. Amateurs tend to dream; professionals consider the realities of a deal.

Find the Market

The prime rule in negotiating is to be a professional. Know what you want to accomplish, know the market, and know the people. Before you sit down at a table to talk, learn all there is to know—about the product, the process, and the individuals. Only then can you find the "hot" button that will turn the other side on. Never walk into any negotiation unprepared.

Negotiation should not be like going on a blind date. You may walk in with great expectations and end up saying to yourself, "Oh, my God. How do I get this evening over with?" Or you can call the person and talk before you commit to an evening. Don't make blind dates in business. In social life, all you blow is a few hours; in business you can blow an entire deal as well as significant amounts of money.

Do your research *before* you begin negotiations. Where is the market? What is the price? If you have someone ready to supply you with goods or services, you can develop some concept of the price, but you can also be way off. If you're dealing with goods, like a pair of shoes, and you are professional in the area, you know the pricing within certain parameters. Your variation isn't going to be more than 5 percent. But what's the value of a patent? What is the worth of a trade name or of an acquisition? If someone is selling his business, your estimation of value could be off by 50 percent. If you are dealing in hard merchandise, the pricing is fairly simple, but if you deal in services, it grows more complex. One lawyer may charge $75 an hour and another may charge $200 but end up being cheaper because he gets much more done in an hour. Such pricing is difficult. How much is a skill worth? How much is the concept worth as opposed to the actual work of putting it together? What is administration worth? It's a wild and woolly judgment call. The only solution is to realize what your goal is and judge its worth for you. There are times when that's as rational an approach as all the research in the world.

Whenever possible, be a counterpuncher. That's a boxing term for, "Let the other guy lead, and when he's made his statement and thrown his punch, see where the opening is." You can see where the deal really is. It's a subtle tactic. When someone says, "Well, Mr. Nadel, what would you offer for this?" my response is, "That's kind of hard to say. What is it that you need?"

"Well, that's not easy to figure out," he says.

"Let me put it this way. If you could write the script for the deal that you want, what would you want?"

By this approach you give the other party the benefit of stating what he wants. But what it reveals is the reality that exists in his mind. Possibly it will be a little exaggerated, because he's going to ask for more than he expects to get, but it gives you a good idea. By the same token, there have been many times that an individual has asked for less than I was willing to pay. By getting him to make a commitment first, it tells you if you're playing in the same game.

Whenever possible, have the other party tell you what he wants, then assess what part of that you can give him. There are times someone will come up with a figure that's so reasonable, you'll know you can make a profit on it and may agree to it right away. If it's a manufactured product, you will have already done your homework to discover what it costs him to make the item and what a fair markup would be.

There's an old adage: "What you know, you know; what you don't know, you'd better listen for." If you want to learn, you have to ask the right questions. More important, you have to be a good listener. Somewhere in the listening process you will find the deal. Discover what the guy knows, what he wants, what his support basis is. Without knowledge, you're operating in the dark.

When I negotiated the purchase of my company from Republic Corporation, for whom I worked at the time, I was armed with knowledge. I knew management was under tremendous pressure from the banks—that they had to get funds or show some progress. And I knew they had to make the deal. Pretty powerful negotiating tools. When I went in, I knew that since my division was one of the few profitable businesses in the company, they wouldn't want to lose their profits. But even stronger was the weapon that I would compete for the same business. Put all that together, and I had the seeds of something workable.

But as important as all those elements was the fact that I understood their tax situation. They had a $40 million tax loss, and if I brought that into the picture, the whole deal would make financial sense to them. It would decrease the price I would have to pay. It all worked to create a deal that benefited everyone.

There were two other reasons why it worked. One is that I wasn't bluffing. When I walked into my negotiation with Republic and said, "Either we strike a deal or I resign and start a competitive company," they knew I wasn't bluffing. If you bluff and get called, you've lost a deal—you could have lost the war. In a negotiation, if I say, "This is my last price," the other party can count on it. If I say I'll do something, he can count on my doing it. There are people who bluff constantly, but I'm not one of them.

There's always the guy who walks in and says, "If you don't give me what I want, I'll quit." If he hears the reply, "Fine. I'll take your resignation right now," the guy will hold up his hand and say "Wait a minute, let's talk about it." It's hard to respect someone like that, let alone take him seriously. If you deliver an ultimatum, you have to be prepared to carry it out. Don't say, "This is my last, absolute bottom price," if it isn't.

The other side of the coin, of course, is to know how to call someone's bluff. Sometimes it's hard to recognize when a person is bluffing; it all depends on whom you're dealing with. Personally, I'd rather deal with a very bright thief than with a very honest idiot. Actually, I'd rather not deal with either, but given a choice, I'd take the thief because I can predict what he's going to do. You need some kind of predictability in people, and you can't predict the actions of a stupid individual if you operate on a logical basis. At least with bright people you know they're not going to do anything to destroy themselves. But with an idiot you never know. He'll tilt at windmills, he'll go after a guy who's six feet seven inches and weighs 300 pounds. He'll jump out of a window or do all manner of irrational things. You never know.

The second additional reason my negotiation with Republic succeeded was because I was negotiating from a position of strength. Never negotiate from a position of need; it's a weak place to be. I was quite willing to leave and start all over again. I had an alternative, and that's a position of strength.

Someone who negotiates out of fear or from a weak position is like the person who puts his house up for sale and then is ecstatic when it sells for his asking price on the second day. All it really means is that he asked too low a price, either because he was dumb or because he desperately needed the deal. A gentleman who once tried to drive down my price on a particular product finally threw his hands up in the air and said, "I can't deal with you."

"Why?" I asked.

"Because you'll live just as well whether you get the deal or not."

Once you get past the point where the difference between making a deal and not making it means bread on your table, you'll be able to negotiate from a much stronger position. Do your homework, know what you want, listen to what the other party wants, maintain a strong position. These are all prerequisites to a successful negotiation.

Visualize the Steps You Plan to Take

There is one powerful negotiating tool that alone can spell the difference between success and failure. I call this technique "visualization." If my readers get nothing else out of this book, this one concept could still alter the way they do business. Visualization means enacting in your mind the logical actions of what you are going to do—before you do it. There is no deal or concept of any importance I do without visualizing it first.

Prior to a negotiation but after all the necessary homework, I turn on the screen in my mind. I enter the room, I see the people, we introduce each other, and we start the conversation. I run the tape all the way through to the end—through the objections, the price levels, the counteroffers, the reactions, the banter, everything. I do the entire meeting in my mind.

Visualization is not thinking about the deal; it is actually doing it. It's like writing your own dream. In your dreams, you don't think about them, you actually *do* them. You can't intellectualize it; that's an entirely different process.

When I go into the actual meeting, I'm entering it for the second time. It doesn't always turn out the way I visualized it, of course. No one could be 100 percent right, and people often slip in surprises. But most often I am 60 or 70 percent right, and that gives me an enormous advantage.

You cannot be prepared for every eventuality, but by going through the deal beforehand you are as well prepared as possible. You know where the deal is, who the players are, and what it will take to consummate it. Once you've finished doing the deal in your head, you're left with a feeling of love, hate, or somewhere in between. A number of times I've actually started to make the deal, gone through the visualization, felt lousy about it, and passed on it.

Discipline is vital. If you are an enormous optimist with a tremendous ego, and you ignore the realities involved, visualization probably won't work for you. When I worked at Republic, my group vice president was a lovely man. There wasn't a down side to him. He viewed everything in the rosy glow of optimism, and he did that company more damage in his nice way than anyone else.

To visualize, you must be a realist, not a pessimist. You must examine all sides of the deal—the up and down, the best case and the worst. You can't say intellectually, "Well, if I fail to do this . . ." or "If I succeed, I'll. . . ." You must go through it as if it were happening. You won't always predict what's going to happen, but you'll prepare yourself by examining it from both ends. You'll go through all the scenarios and assess your odds. You'll be prepared.

Visualization is something anyone with a disciplined mind can accomplish. If you want to ask your boss for a raise, sit quietly for a few minutes and play it through in your mind. Say what you want to say, predict his responses, listen to what he says, and come back with what you want to say. It didn't sound good? Go back to the beginning and do it over again.

It's like being a great performer. Actors never go on stage without rehearsing their act. They have worked at it, hard. They have sung the song, made the movements, said the lines—over and over. But the test is when they actually go out there and do it. The performance sounds as if they are doing it for the first time.

Why not do the same in business? Practice. Rehearse. Just as a great actor walks effortlessly onto the stage and doesn't appear to be acting, so you can walk effortlessly into a negotiation and know how it will turn out. It's professionalism in a different arena, and it is well worth the discipline it takes.

Lose a Battle!

You don't have to win every battle, as long as you win the war. Business, like everything else, is a series of wins and losses. Sometimes it even pays to lose a battle.

Recently, I hired a designer on an hourly rate, with a ceiling price on the project. About one-fourth of the way through the project I knew he couldn't do it, so I cut off the deal, as allowed in our agreement. Over and above his fees, he charged me an extra $600. This was completely unjustified, so I didn't pay it. I sent him a polite letter, restating the terms of our agreement. Shortly after, I got a notice to appear in Pasadena's small claims court—a city some 30 miles from where I live and work. The designer was claiming his $600. I lost the battle, and I paid him $600. Sure, I felt I was right, but I didn't want to go to Pasadena. I couldn't afford to spend a day in small claims court, and I didn't want to aggravate myself further.

Battles such as these must be relegated to the unimportant position they deserve. I could have been self-righteous. I could have stood on principle and shown him he was picking on the wrong guy. I could have gone to Pasadena and fought it out. But what would I have accomplished? Would I have elevated myself in my own eyes?

No, I would rather lose the battle. I'm not going out of my way to damage this designer, but I will never do business with him again. And if anyone ever calls me for a reference, they will get the full story. End of battle.

In Japan I found a book called *The Three Bamboos*. Three bamboos was the trademark of an old trading family, whose business knowledge had passed from father to son for centuries. The book explains why the bamboo was the family logo. They could have used an oak, which is solid and strong, but a storm or strong wind can knock an oak tree down. But no matter how powerful the wind nor how far over the bamboo sways, it always returns to an upright position. The bamboo can bend, but never break.

Americans are like oaks. "I'm strong. I'll stand here. Throw your bolts of lightning and blow your winds; I'll stand." There's no such oak. They all fall sooner or later.

This doesn't mean you must give up your independence or lose your integrity. But realize that you can't swim against the tide. Pay attention to overall conditions and go with them. The winds blow one way and you export; they blow in the opposite direction and you import. When you are influenced by something as powerful as the tides or major economic trends, know that you cannot change them. Learn to live with them. That's the trick.

This advice applies even to seemingly small things sometimes. It relates to what I call "rigid flexibility." In negotiations it's important to have an amount of flexibility. You want to be able to give a little to satisfy the deal, but you can't give away the store. The point of balance is attained through rigidity *and* flexibility. Don't be a rubber band, but be willing to stretch sometimes.

If you lose a battle, do it gracefully, keeping in mind that the battle is only a small part of the war. Then move on to the next battle, perhaps wiser. If you are rigid as an oak tree, however, you may not only lose the battle but also destroy yourself. Judge how important the matter is before you're willing to be felled. There are times when unrestrained ego can lead you straight down the mouth of the cannon.

Ego

If fear of failure hinders success, the reverse—inflated ego— is just as detrimental. Ego can lose battles for you, damage negotiations, and (if you keep thinking you can do things you are totally incapable of doing) keep you trying and failing. Someone asked me recently if I had ever made mistakes. My answer was, "Come over and I'll show them to you. I have a warehouse full of them."

Nobody bats a thousand, but I've known prominent business people who never admit a mistake. I've seen numbers of people fall in love with products they've created, instead of putting them on the closeout rack. I've seen them pull out all the stops and increase efforts and advertising expenditures, trying to sell a dog. When I asked a designer in Italy for certain elements in a product, he said he could easily bring it off because he was a great designer. He never did; it just wasn't within his capabilities. But his ego didn't let him admit that.

Ego is a terrible thing. You can make commitments you're in no position to make, buy things you can't afford, say things you don't mean. Someone once worked for me who had a fragile ego and a great deal of bravado. It was very easy for anyone in an adversarial position to take him out for a great dinner, get him loaded, and tell him everything he wanted to hear. He went into every deal trying to prove how smart he was. That's not the object of a deal.

If you are negotiating with someone who has an oversized ego, make it work for you. "I don't think you're capable of making this for the price," you assert.

"Are you kidding?" he says "I've got the best operation in the world."

"Nah. It's impossible for you to do it that way."

"I can do it! I'll show you." And he'll prove he can do it, because he's the sharpest operator around.

Ever since I lost my first fistfight at school, I realized that as tough as you are, there's someone somewhere who's tougher. As smart as you are, there's always someone smarter—and there's a pretty good chance you are going to run into him. When that happens, back off. Submerge your ego and be analytical. It's a lot safer, and a whole lot more profitable.

Discipline

Negotiation requires discipline, not only in your actions but also in your thoughts. People who think there are only one or two solutions to a problem lack the mental discipline to create solutions. The reality is that there are dozens, perhaps hundreds, of solutions. It takes discipline during a negotiation not to accept in your mind what someone else has decided are the only alternatives.

One of the main products of undisciplined thinking is impatience. "Take it or leave it," people say, or "Fish or cut bait." It's a bad attitude in the international market. Impatience, a particularly American flaw, puts you at a disadvantage.

In the Orient in particular, there is always plenty of time. In April 1985, we started a deal in China that terribly excited us. In April 1987, it still hadn't been executed. The Chinese don't think in terms of a deal—or a year. They think in centuries.

American businessmen are often just too impatient to construct a proper deal, so the deal gets watered down. Look at the Japanese government. They say yes to everything, but do they execute? They have tap danced for five years over the matter of a U.S. trade aggreement, and we still haven't gotten anything firm. They assure our government they are going to look into it, but nothing concrete happens. In the meantime, their delaying tactics have certainly enhanced their economy. American businessmen have to learn how to cope with these attitudes. God knows, you can't change them. You don't have to play exactly the same game, but you have to understand the rules.

Learn the habits of the cultures you do business with. This takes discipline, however. Discipline is doing what you have to do, no matter how distasteful, to attain a goal. People who want to be loved by everyone usually end up being loved by no one. They move from being a wimp to being an autocrat. Just like everything else in life, there is a comfort zone somewhere in between.

When I was just starting out, I was working day and night, seven days a week, passing up a lot of social invitations in the process. A good friend said, "Boy, I'd never work that hard. That's ridiculous, Jack. It just isn't worth it." But that was my discipline. Years later I'm not working seven days a week. I work hard, but according to the schedule I choose. And this man is still struggling to make a living. He's doing the same thing he's been doing for years, but it's becoming tougher now because he's competing with younger guys in the marketplace.

I decided to make it while I was young—while I had the strength, the guts, and the energy. I didn't want to be doing it when I was older. The difference between us was discipline.

Discipline in thoughts, in actions, in achieving product standards, and in enforcement of policies are crucial in business. Just as an army moves on discipline, so does a business. Without it you have no organization of any size, no team, and ultimately no business.

Greed

Greed can blow deals, destroy relationships, and ruin businesses. It's what gives businessmen a bad name. And it is totally unneccessary. If there's not enough fair profit in your line of business, move on to something new. Greed is what makes you try to wring the last drop of blood out of someone and incur his undying resentment. It's what makes you try for that last iota of profit and destroy the negotiation.

A perfect example of greed occurred when I was with Republic Corporation. All the companies acquired by Republic had been exchanged for unregistered stock, which couldn't be traded for a specific number of years unless the company went through the time and expense of registering a certain amount to be sold on the open market. From the time my company had been acquired the stock had risen from about $40 to about $70 a share. I and a number of the other division presidents who had formerly owned businesses and who now had large holdings of Republic stock went to the chairman of the board, Gerald Block. We asked him to register some stock so that we could sell it and gain some liquidity.

"No. It's not time yet," he said. "The stock is going to go up further."

We told him the stock had already moved up really high, and that we'd like to get some of our cash out. Yes, it might go up further, but we'd be quite happy at the present price. Block refused, saying that when the stock hit $100 a share he would register the stock. It never did hit $100. The stock went to $90 and then began a long, deathly slide. Over a period of time, it went all the way down to $1.50. Because of one man's greed, a group of disgruntled division presidents saw their security go right down the drain.

You'll never go broke taking a profit. The individual who thinks he can always buy at the bottom of the market and sell at the top is a fool. None of us are smart enough to predict the tops and bottoms. Even though you may kick yourself later for selling too early or buying too late, if you can make a profit somewhere in between, you did fine.

Greedy people keep going for the big hit. It's like leaving your money on the crap table. You can keep throwing naturals, but all you have to do is throw craps once and you're out of the game. Greed is also the motive that makes you take that one step from rational behavior into the "twilight zone." It can make you believe something that is entirely unbelieveable or walk down a road you have no business being on. This is what all con men depend on.

Not being a paragon of virtue, I'm as guilty as the next man. It began out of necessity. We had bought a 200,000-square-foot building on ten acres in the Marina del Rey area of Los Angeles. We paid $13 million for it. We ran into problems with the financing and wound up paying 18 percent for the mortgage. This meant that the interest alone was costing us about $2 million a year. It was in 1981, and the prime rate was at its peak.

There were a lot of stories circulating at the time about Arab money—petrodollars. Arab potentates had treasures buried in the sand outside their tents. Billions and billions of dollars. Now I don't normally respond to rumors, but I got this one from a very reliable source, a banker in New York. He had personal contact with a particular Arab, he said, and vouched for him. The sheik was in Frankfurt. Since I had to go to Europe anyway, I thought I'd look into it.

I told my banker in Los Angeles about it, and he simply frowned and said, "There's no such thing, Jack. Forget it." I chose to ignore his advice. The need was there. I had to have better financing. All around me, people in real estate and business were going broke trying to service their debt, and I didn't want to be one of them. From Los Angeles, I called the sheik's representative in Germany and told him I was looking for $10 million.

Yes, they were interested in American real estate. Yes, they were interested in doing business with me. Yes, they'd be willing to lend me $10 million at 10 percent interest, the man said. This was phenomenal. Suddenly I could knock

$800,000 a year off my servicing charges. Not only that, I could lend that money at slightly under the going rate and get in to the money business to make a fortune! Ah, greed.

The arrangements were right out of a spy novel. Everything was arranged in a cloak-and-dagger style. The sheik would see me at such-and-such a place on the outskirts of Frankfurt on a particular day. But I had to be at a certain place at a specific time, and I'd receive a telephone call and then someone would meet me.

I was at the Carlton Hotel in Cannes, France, when the sheik's representative called. He told me a limousine would meet me at the airport at 10 A.M. the next day and take me to an address outside of Frankfurt. My associate, Harold Holland, was with me, and we had a hell of a time trying to get a flight to Frankfurt. Everything direct was fully booked. Finally, we managed to get a flight that went to Frankfurt via Zurich. There was a long wait between flights and the normal 55-minute trip took six hours.

The limousine was there. It took us to what was literally an armed enclave outside Frankfut. There were guards with guns, vicious dogs, and barbed wire on the walls surrounding an ancient mansion. We were taken to the living room, ornately furnished and with high ceilings. After we had waited for a while, the sheik's representative entered. He was an overweight, slightly unsavory looking, pompous American who reminded me of the actor Sidney Greenstreet.

"Yes, we can do this for you, but we have to arrange for the money to come out of Geneva," he explained.

During my earlier telephone conversations, they had said the loan would cost five points. For $10 million it would cost us $500,000—still a great deal. I agreed, willingly. Now the man added, "There will be loan fees, of course. Not too much. Initially it will just be two hundred thousand. The rest can be paid later."

"I'll be very willing to pay all five points after we have the ten million—not before," I said firmly.

"That shows a definite lack of good faith," he said, his feelings obviously hurt.

"I'm sorry, but those are my rules," I insisted.

"Fine, fine," he said. "We can deal with that later."

He began to take down all the information: the location of the land, the history of our firm, and everything else. "That'll be all," he said when he had all the details he required. "You'll hear from us next Tuesday at 9 A.M."

We were dismissed. We never saw the sheik, although a lady dressed in a veil once walked by. The limousine took us back to the airport, and we flew back to France.

At precisely 9 A.M. on Tuesday, I received a telephone call from the sheik's representative. "All is in order. We can transfer the money to your account immediately. But there's just one thing," he said.

"What's that?" I asked.

"There's a small fee involved. Only fifty thousand. But this must be paid as a transfer fee. Just send us a bank draft, and as soon as we receive that, we'll transfer the ten million."

"I'll be willing to pay that as soon as my bank verifies receipt of the ten million," I said.

"No, I'm afraid those costs must be paid first, as a show of good faith."

"I'd be happy to place the amount in escrow, to be released as soon as receipt of the ten million is verified," I said.

"No, it must be paid beforehand."

The temptation to put out a mere $50,000 to get $10 million at eight points below the going interest rate was extreme, to say the least. Nevertheless, I passed.

There never was any money. I never met anyone who ever got any money. The whole thing was a giant scam. There were countless dozens of otherwise bright business people who got ripped off for fees ranging from $50,000 to as much as $1 million.

There's an old saying, "Never get into a card game with a guy named Slick." It's an adage that normally intelligent people willingly ignore under the influence of greed. When people get taken over the coals in deals like this one, the motivating factor is always greed.

There are fabulously good deals in the world, or so I've heard. If someone approaches you with one someday, it may even be true. But examine it very, very hard, and never put out anything up front. Never pay out the money before you get your money in the bank. Greed makes people irrational. The fact of the matter is, "There ain't no free falafel."

Negotiate an honest deal. Ignore the temptations of greed; push aside the impulses of ego. Do your homework, visualize the negotiation beforehand, and make the only deal that really works—an honest one in which everyone wins.

7

Partners—And Other People

Let's start with one premise that's true: All business is personal. People do business with people they want to do business with. And most of the time, people deal with the people they deserve.

Finding your trading partners is as important as anything else you do. After you've found your product, figured your deal, and determined whether it can work, the most important part of the transaction is the person (or people) with whom you deal. This is true whether you are a manufacturer or a service company seeking to export goods or services. Theoretically, a deal can appear to be the best in the world, but if the people are not right, you can fall flat on your face.

How do you qualify people on other continents, in other countries? Well, apart from the steps mentioned in Chapter 3 with regard to checking with banks, suppliers, customers, and so forth, it is a process that continues throughout your business. You don't just qualify someone once, then hope for the best. It's something you have to monitor constantly. You can have an associate or trading partner who does quite well for a time, but then he can change. He may go through some personal crisis, his business might shift direction, or some part of his setup can change in another way.

Determine the integrity level and work patterns of an individual with whom you are thinking of dealing. Gut feelings play an important part here, of course, but sometimes it takes time. My mother used to say, "Every pot finds its cover." What you do is find people to work with who mirror your own standards and feelings.

I employ many salesmen, and it is amazing how the detail-oriented salesmen only sell to detail-oriented companies. One of my most productive salesmen spent as much time as possible at the racetrack. But he sold mainly to people who went to the races. It follows, down the line. Whether people are quality conscious, sloppy, or somewhere in between, their basic work habits follow along similar lines.

"Good Enough" People

I am often asked how I find and keep a great staff. The fact is, my employees like their jobs, enjoy what they are doing, and are not capable of doing a bad job. They want to do the best possible work, and they have a quality orientation. The people to avoid are the "good enough" people. They consider everything they do "good enough." They are never going to produce a superior product, and they will never turn it out on time or live up to what you need. "Good enough" people are well meaning, lazy, and to be avoided.

People who take pride in what they do have quality standards. Their standards are not *your* quality standards; you can't give them those. They belong to the individual. Likewise, I have discovered that I can't give a manufacturer who pays no attention to quality or detail any incentive to be better. We once owned a company that manufactured pens. We were doing well, except that we were unable to produce a quality product. The problem was the division manager. Time and again I'd say to him, "The pens don't write properly, the action doesn't work well, the finish isn't good, the packaging is lousy, the presentation is wrong, the catalogs don't do the jobs. . . ." He swore he'd try harder.

I think he did try, but it didn't matter. It just wasn't within him. He couldn't do it. When he looked at the factory, he didn't see the quality of the product. He saw only the number of pens manufactured per hour. That was his basic orientation, and he couldn't be broken of it.

Finally, I was exasperated enough to tell him it was time for a parting of the ways. It just wasn't working. "I'd like to give you ninety days' off-the-cuff notice," I said. "It's not official notice, but I want you to start looking for a job. I know it's a lot easier to find a job when you have one."

He couldn't believe it. "I get along great with you. What's the problem?" he said.

"No, you don't," I replied. "You're not doing what I'm paying you to do, and I can't be a policeman forever. Let's just call it quits."

"But I love the pen company. Let me buy it," he said.

I gave him 90 days to put together a group to buy the company or to find another job. After 90 days he was still there, continuing his job as if the conversation had never occurred. Finally, I said I was going to give him official notice.

"You can't do that," he said. "The union is behind me. You'll have a strike if you terminate me. The union guy is my buddy, and he's an old bone-breaker. He doesn't play around."

There was a threat in there somewhere, but I ignored it and sent him his official notice. Sure enough, I got a call from the union asking for a meeting. I met them in my suite at New York's Pierre Hotel. The union man must have been six foot, 7 inches.

"Hey, why'd you wanna fire him?" he asked.

"Simple. I don't like the way he works, and we're losing money," I replied.

"So what happens when we pull a strike?"

"I don't understand," I said. "He's company management and you're union. You're supposed to protect jobs. Why are you here talking about him? He's not union."

"Yeah, but he's an old friend of mine," the guy said.

"I can't help that," I said.

"Why'd you wanna fire him?" he repeated belligerently.

"He's doing a lousy job. We're putting out a shitty product, and the company is losing money. I've got no other reason."

He squinted at me. "I wanna talk to you alone," he said. "Let's go to the bathroom."

Like an idiot, I went to the bathroom with him. "Are you serious?" he asked, closing the door behind us. "You really wanna fire him?"

The man's bulky body filled the bathroom. He towered over me. I had visions of my body being discovered floating in the tub. But I didn't show my fear. "Yes. I'm going to fire him," I said.

"Where you from?" he asked.

"Lower East Side, just like you," I said.

He looked at me, and then his face cracked into the semblance of a grin. "I like you. Fuck him! He's out! You got no trouble with me, Jack. I'm your buddy." I heaved a sigh of relief as we shook hands.

A Quality Orientation

People are either quality oriented or not. This particular manager was price and quantity oriented, and there's no way he could be otherwise. By the same token, I've been to companies who turn out quality products, and I've asked for a lower price. They can't reduce the price because of the time and effort they put into their quality. If quality is secondary, go to a price house. If quality is important, then go to the quality house and be prepared to pay a premium. And remember that in all companies, business policy travels from the top down. It is always a reflection of the head man.

Part of my sales pitch to clients has been that we're not the cheapest outfit on the street. But if they want results, then we're their people—and it's the best value in the world. If they want to shop around for the best price, I say, "Forget it. We're not even in the ballpark, and we don't want to bid.

That's not our business." I found that, to suit my personality, it was just as easy to sell a quality program as to sell a price program. I chose to go with quality, and that's the type of people I hire.

There are fine points to this matter of judging people. For example, you need people with differing abilities. Always look for reliability, honesty, and integrity, but people need not always have the same values you do or have every ability in the book. If I approach a manufacturer who is quality oriented, I don't necessarily need him to be creative; that's my job. All I want from him is to make the product according to my specifications, provide quality at a fair price, and deliver it on time. He's only entitled to so much of a margin, because that's all he's providing: merchandise to specification. There are many people out there who can do that. It's a matter of supply and demand.

On the other hand, if I want someone to sell my merchandise in a foreign country, I look for something entirely different. I still want reliability, honesty, and integrity, but I also want creativity. If he isn't creative, he won't be able to sell in the competitive marketplace. This person is also entitled to a higher share of the profits. He's usually on commission, and if he doesn't sell, he doesn't make money.

Creative people are almost irreplaceable, while those who provide mechanical functions number in the thousands. One of our divisions, Art-Mold/Pierre Cardin, was started in 1954. It began with the name Art-Mold because we sold molded products: key tags, luggage tags, and the like. But from day one, we never owned a single molding machine. Why? Because in the real world there are hundreds of custom molders. Give them your mechanical drawings and specifications, and they can mold anything you want.

I don't need the overhead or the concern of keeping equipment busy. All I have to worry about is making a product that's going to sell. We create the product, assemble it, imprint it, package it, and do whatever else is necessary, but we don't have to be in the molding business, too. All the molder does is mold; he takes no risk. We create the product and the marketplace and thus are entitled to more. It's the law of supply and demand.

When I'm trying to find people with whom to operate my business—be they employees, makers, sellers, or brokers—I judge each by the different standards needed to get the job done properly. The same principles apply, whether I'm doing business locally or internationally.

Checking Up—Long Distance

Because of geographical factors, it becomes a little more difficult to judge people overseas, but basically the situation is the same. Accommodate the differences, and realize that it might take a little longer.

If I find a maker for a given product, say, in France, I can easily get a list of people he's been making things for. Then I write or talk to them. In talking to his customers, I approach it as I do when hiring an important person and checking references. "It's always nice to say good things," I say, "but I'd like you to understand that this conversation is strictly off the record, and I'd really like to know what your experience has been with this individual. And I'd like you to extend the same courtesy to me as I would to you, if the positions were reversed. I'm sure if you called me you'd like to know if the man delivered on time, if the quality standards were good, and so on."

That way I get the truth. It's the same, whether I'm contracting with a supplier or hiring an individual. But I never take just one person's word. There may be some bitterness or misunderstanding involved. If I call five people, however, and five people say, "He's a real nice guy, but he hasn't delivered anything on time in the past year," then I know he is either a chronic late deliverer or an early promiser.

The element that no business person likes is surprise. This is particularly true when dealing long distance. On a local basis, if something promised doesn't arrive, you can pick up the phone and say, "Charlie, what's happening?" But if you are dealing with someone in Japan, you have a complex problem. So you really have to be able to count on the people with whom you work.

The qualifying process is continuous. You never stop because a company never stops. If it's a big company, people change and so do their standards. If it's a small company, there are totally different problems. It takes time to weed out those who have been good, bad, or mediocre. You find that certain makers do better with certain kinds of products, that some have small faults and others have large.

If you think a maker has a big potential for you, start with a small order. Give them a delivery date, see how well you communicate, and build to having a new trading partner. At first, you'll have just a supplier, but if it works out, and you do it often enough, you'll have added a valuable trading partner.

Suppliers

Once you find someone you can work with, don't get hung up on the idea that he's your only source. Exclusivity is one of the easiest traps to fall into. When you find an exclusive source who says he'll fill all your needs, it seems very attractive. Unfortunately, often that source is incapable of doing just that, and you wind up with a "sweetheart deal."

There are many variations of the sweetheart deal, and none are good. A supplier may feel you are at his mercy and take advantage of the situation. Another may send nice gifts and football tickets, but not be too careful how he charges you. Yet another may ingratiate himself with the people who do the buying and furnish them with *whatever* it is they want. (This can range from something as innocuous as football tickets to something as terrible as cash kickbacks.) If left too long in the hands of one person, this situation tends to disintegrate into a one-on-one social relationship in which prices aren't even questioned. And that's a dangerous situation to get into.

Once again, the qualifying process must be continuous. Let's look at it in the ways you make money, particularly in the buying process. For instance, you make money three ways: by selling, by running a tight company without excess overhead, and by buying.

You make almost as much money buying as you do selling. The art of buying is the most overlooked segment of business. For example, I operate on the premise that I always want my supplier to make a good profit on me—not an excessive profit, but a good profit, so that I'm an important customer to him. It's up to me to understand, among other things, what his costs are so that I can determine that range. And even more important, I always have to remember to run a check on his competitors to make sure he is still competitive. That's my prime rule of buying.

I had a very good friend in the same business. I operated in Los Angeles and he was in Chicago, so we weren't competitors. We would compare notes and sometimes even buy cooperatively to get a better deal with suppliers. Once, I was buying a product he never did much business with, but when he saw how well I was doing, he decided to give it another try. I gave him the name of a supplier—another good friend. He contacted the supplier and, without buying a single piece, negotiated a better price than I was paying after doing a great deal of business with that supplier.

It shocked me. I realized I had a situation that needed correction, and it taught me a valuable lesson. Not only do you have to constantly qualify the people you do business with, but you have to do the same for yourself. Did I get fat and soft, taking on a layer of flab that made me noncompetitive? Was someone giving out orders without double-checking the company's needs? Putting all that aside, I had to make sure I was doing the job. If any part of my operation doesn't work, it's my fault and I'd better find out why and where it isn't working.

It's best to develop a fair but tough reputation for buying. While you allow your supplier to make a good profit, you keep it from being excessive by making sure he is competitive. And you don't try to get the last drop of blood out of him. If you drive your supplier down to the lowest price he can give, the relationship won't last. It's a balancing act among price, quality, and competitiveness, but somewhere in there is a steady, level spot. The grasping for that spot will show you that buying is part science, part art, dependent on both practical knowledge and intuition.

A Difference of Opinion

My first job in the specialty advertising business ended in part over the issue of people. I was working for the firm of Seabury & Company, and I was considered the boy wonder. After six months, I was appointed sales manager. By the end of the first year, I was responsible for 30 percent of the company's business.

I was free to hire the salesmen I wanted, but had no jurisdiction over those who were already working for Seabury. All the salesmen were independent contractors, the theory being that you hired as many salesmen as you could, knowing that although they wouldn't last, a few would come back with orders. As I started to build a professional sales force—carefully hiring and training each individual—I realized it would be impossible to develop a class operation. My prestige salespeople had to work alongside anyone who could carry a sample.

My frustration grew. At the end of three years, it came to a head. My boss and I had a tremendous difference of opinion on how to operate the business. I wanted to discharge everyone and start from scratch to hire full-time salespeople who would work exclusively for our company. The president, Eric Seabury, was aghast. "You can't do that. We'd lose all our income," he protested.

"You simply can't run a Tiffany and a Woolworth under the same roof," I said. "We can't be half this and half that." And yet, despite our vast differences, Eric offered me a partnership in their operation.

There were already three partners. Eric actually ran the business with an active partner, and there was a silent partner in New York. The deal they offered me was to buy 25 percent of the company for the book value of $25,000, plus a factor of $25,000 extra for goodwill. Although it was a relatively small business, my initial investment still had to be in excess of $25,000, with another $25,000 to come a year later.

I had wanted this offer for a long time, but as I examined it I realized it was inequitable and too unrealistic for me. I would constantly be outvoted, but, more important, we would always disagree because of our different concepts about how the business should operate. I had pretty much made up my mind to pass.

It was our third meeting in a week, and it was the day to make a decision. Eric and I met down the street from the office in a room at the Mayfair Hotel. The Mayfair had seen better days, I remember. The room was musty, the beds were lumpy, and the two overstuffed chairs sagged under our weight. I told Eric I was going to pass. He always appeared jovial, but now his face turned a bright red.

"How can you turn it down, Jack?" he asked. "Here's your big opportunity to be part of a proven, growing business. You'll be fourth partner with an equal share. We've talked about it for a year, finally decided to let you in, and you say no! Are you nuts?"

"But—" I began.

"Jack, don't you understand?" he interrupted. "This year you get in. Next year we may buy out the other two. Then there's just you and me. Equal partners—fifty-fifty. It's a great deal for you."

My heart pounded. Here I was with my boss, and he was all but pleading with me to accept an offer I had wanted to receive for over a year.

"It just won't work," I said. "You show an inflated book value and then you add twenty-five thousand for goodwill. I don't have twenty-five thousand to pay for the stock, and even if I did, it's still a bad deal. Where's my goodwill? After all, I wrote over thirty percent of the total business last year myself!"

"Jack, you're just twenty-nine years old," Eric said, exasperated. "You don't understand. Trust me. Together we can burn up the turf. You need me for my experience, and I need you for your sales ability and youth. We could make one hell of a team."

My throat tightened and my eyes blurred. "Eric," I said. "Let's part friends. For one-half the money I could start my own small business. I would like to have you as a partner, but I just can't accept this deal. I've worked for you up to this minute. Now, I'm going to strike out on my own."

I stuck out my hand. Eric looked at it for a long second, then shoved it away angrily. "If you don't take the deal, I'll blackball you with every supplier," he said. "This is your last chance." My knees shook as I slowly turned away and walked out of the hotel room. The meeting was over.

Eric's enraged face kept reappearing in my mind as I drove home. It was hard to believe we had come to a parting of the ways. I had great affection for him, and we had become close friends. Eric and his wife, Miriam, were about 20 years older than Elly and I, but we had a lot of fun and had taken trips together as couples. Now it was over, and his bitterness would grow.

Elly took one look at me when she greeted me at the door and saw the meeting had been tough. We had discussed it the night before and both had agreed that the price would have to be reduced for the deal to make any sense. "What if they won't make this concession?" I had finally asked, voicing my fear. Elly hesitated only a moment. "Well, we'll just have to start our own business," she said.

The next morning Elly went looking for office space while I delivered the last orders I had taken to Seabury and collected my final check. I was greeted at the office by cold stares from the management and warm handshakes from the salesmen. Eric refused to see me as I returned my order books and samples and said my last good-byes.

Elly found a tiny office on Wilshire Boulevard in Beverly Hills. It was 12 feet square, barely big enough to hold the two used desks. Elly had a portable typewriter—our first piece of equipment. She would run the office. She is efficient and bright, and has marvelous taste. I had full confidence in her ability. We kissed for luck, and I asked, "Are you scared?"

"Not at all," she answered. "You can do anything you want. I know you'll be great!" And so, on January 10, 1953, when Dwight D. Eisenhower was about to start his first term as president, I was about to start my first business.

I'm convinced that if I had accepted Eric's deal, or some variation of it, I would have been miserable and frustrated. My imagination and desire for work would never have been allowed to extend itself to its full potential. Since then, even through the ups and downs of business, I have never regretted the decision. And I have never again had to compromise my standards about the people I hire or work with.

Partners

While finding trading partners is important, even more important is finding something as intimate as honest-to-God business partners. This is business's equivalent of a marriage, and, like marriage these days, the divorce rate is high. Very few partnerships really work. Too many dissolve in argument and recrimination.

I have been very lucky. I have not one, not two, but three partners. It's tough enough for two partners to work together, but four partners are a geometrical potential for trouble. And we've had it. We've been through good times and bad, had stormy sessions, and resolved many problems, but it has always been amazing to the outside world that we've been able to stay together and maintain such close, personal relations.

In 1968, I sold Jack Nadel, Inc., to Republic Corporation and became head of the Advertising Specialty Companies of Republic, already discussed in Chapter 6. By 1970, we had made some acquisitions and formed Measured Marketing Services. In 1973, we bought back the subsidiary and formed a new corporation, Measured Marketing Services, Inc. Today it has four divisions: Krupp/Taylor, an advertising agency with its own production facilities, dealing only in direct mail; Jack Nadel, Inc., direct response promotions; Art-Mold/Pierre Cardin, a specialty advertising manufacturer and the importer and distributor of Pierre Cardin writing instruments; and MMS Design, responsible for promotion and product development.

I have been asked how the four of us have managed to stay together all these years, and I have replied that it is because each of the divisions are run autonomously. Each partner has complete authority to run his division, except for certain key decisions—such as capital expenditures and other major moves—that must come from the corporate office. But the day-to-day operation stays right in the division.

There's more to it than that, of course. Just as important is the caliber of the people involved. I met my first partner when he was born. And it's indeed fortunate that my brother Marty turned out to be one of the most talented individuals to come to my organization.

Marty built his reputation on the basis of knowledge. He became the expert in promotion for the financial community in southern California. Every time he approached a financial institution, he knew what they could do and what they couldn't do. In 1970, when I moved up Republic's corporate ladder to head Measured Marketing Services, Marty took over as president of Jack Nadel, Inc. He had to contend with my reputation at first. Everything he did in his new job was criticized with "Jack wouldn't have done it this way." Marty had the good sense to create his own image. He'd reply, "No, but that's the way I'm doing it." He made an indelible stamp on the company, while denying none of the concepts that created the company. When we made the buy-back, Marty became one of the partners and continued as president of one of the main divisions, as well as vice president of marketing for Measured Marketing Services, Inc.

My second partner was the brother of Julian Holland, who started Art-Mold Company. Unfortunately, Julian was suffering from Parkinson's disease and wanted to sell his company. I had done business with the company for years and knew it well. When Republic was looking for acquisitions, it became a prime candidate.

The acquisition was completed very quickly, with both a sense of elation and sadness. The sadness was that Julian had to sell because he was incapable of carrying on, and the elation was over the fact that we had bought a very good company. Since Julian was going to retire, the obvious choice for president was Harold Holland, his younger brother. Harold proved to be every bit as good at running an efficient company, but in addition, he had a special talent and knowledge of selling to the specialty distributor. He added the ingredient of a true sales personality who had a real understanding of his customers. When the buy-back took place a few years later he became the vice president of manufacturing for Measured Marketing Services and president of Art-Mold, and a logical partner in the company.

My meeting with the third man who was to become a partner involved some corporate infighting, which is something I rarely get involved in. I was president of a division of Republic and overseeing two other companies. At the time, conglomerates were in disrepair and Republic was a typical conglomerate. As I've mentioned earlier in this book, the stock was dropping rapidly and they were concerned.

The chairman of Republic announced to me their intention to split various parts of the company from the main body and take them into separate public issues, thereby raising funds and increasing the company's visibility. He asked if I'd be interested in heading up a new subsidiary consisting of all the marketing and advertising parts of Republic. I agreed, with a few conditions, and a couple of weeks later they told me I had the job.

Republic had acquired a direct-mail company—the Krupp Organization—a year earlier. What I didn't know at the time was that the president of Krupp had been interviewed for the new job as well. It came as a complete surprise when he resigned in anger over the decision to give me the position.

The first meeting of the divisions that were going to become the new Measured Marketing Services was set for virtually the same day Krupp's president resigned. In his stead came a man by the name of Bob Buckingham. Bob, it turned out, was the kind of man who accepted nothing at face value. He was suspicious of me right from the start. He raised a quizzical eyebrow every time I spoke. I knew I'd have to prove myself. I guess I did, because over the next year we became fast friends. We have proved our capabilities to each other over and over again. When we bought out the company, Bob became my third partner.

At the time we took the company out of Republic we were doing $13 million a year. Today, because of the four partners involved and all the people who came with us, we do in excess of $100 million dollars. And the past 13 years have been an absolutely magnificent experience.

My partners are three very different men. They do have five things in common, however. The first common factor is dedication, second is intelligence, third is a common work ethic, fourth is that they are absolute experts in their fields and take a backseat to no one, and fifth is that each respects each other's abilities. We like each other as people and trust each other implicitly.

My friends and partners are such that we can argue vociferously in private, but the decision is made with one voice. There is never a hint of dissension. We march as one group. If there is disagreement or an impasse, then all heads turn to me as chairman of the company and the decision is made. And that's the end of the discussion. This isn't done with any subservience whatsoever. But as hard, pragmatic businessmen, all three of my partners know that a decision has to be made. It may not be their decision, but when we leave the room, no one else ever knows who took an opposing side.

We also decided that there would be no more partners. It's a closed story. No matter how high powered the new employee or how much he asked for equity, the answer is no. We'll treat them marvelously, pay them well, give them percentages, but there's no equity. This policy has caused the loss of a few good people, but by the same token we never give any one we hire false promises. If there's a disappointment, it's up front. We have a closed four-way marriage that works because of the chemistry among us.

Another interesting fact is that we are all salesmen. Our divisions aren't headed by accountants or administrators, but by aggressive salesmen. Nothing happens until you sell something, and each partner knows that. And each is capable of doing more selling than anyone who works for him. It's a great morale booster, like soldiers in a battle who see the general heading a platoon. It has a way of inspiring people and keeping everything vibrant.

The whole area of choosing people is absolutely critical. I'm often asked how I'm able to do as much as I do. It's only because I've got a sensational group of people around me— not only my partners, but the people we employ.

I believe in making the company more difficult to replace than the individual. Many businesses are concerned that if top salesmen or key executives leave it will cripple their company. I put it another way. The key executive or salesman should be convinced that if he leaves, although it will be traumatic, we can replace him, but he will never be able to replace the company.

Usually an employee leaves a company because the company has left him. If you can get people working with as much information as they can have, satisfied that they're well paid and motivated by future rewards, you have good employees. One of the prime functions of a company is not only to build profits, but to provide opportunity. It's up to management to provide opportunity at each level, so everyone has something to look forward to. And then give them all the extras you possibly can. People don't only work for money; they also work for applause, a pat on the back.

So, how do you choose people? You choose them by trial and error, by capabilities, by genuine talent, and by chemistry—which takes us back to gut feelings. I look at qualified people and either say I like them or it's not going to work. It's as simple as that. I make my decision and eliminate the problem before it starts. Never go against what your gut tells you. To some it may seem unfair or terribly shortsighted, but it works.

You know how good your partners are when times are rough, when one division is pulling another down financially and putting a strain on the rest of the company. That's when the character of the individual and the character of the company come out. This is true of long-term business partners as well as trading partners. The strength of the relationship has to override temporary distractions. If you survive, you just get stronger.

Partners in Crisis!

In November 1982, Measured Marketing Services was in big trouble. A number of elements had combined to bring the situation about. We had purchased property in Marina del Rey, California, for our direct-mail company. We moved from about 48,000 square feet to 200,000 square feet, with a comparable increase in overhead. Our rent alone went from approximately $30,000 a month to $150,000 a month.

Nothing costs as much as you expect. It's usually more. Part of our move involved merging our direct-mail plant in Portland, Oregon, with the company in California. Taylor in Portland and Krupp in Los Angeles became Krupp-Taylor in the new facility.

We gave generous termination pay to the Portland staff and also set up our own agency to help relocate those who didn't want to come to Los Angeles. This was very expensive, but we felt an obligation. And then, when we decided to remodel the new building, our cost projections were way under the actual. We spent much more than expected.

We had a plan to accommodate this enormous expansion. We were moving the direct-mail company from being simply a letter shop to a full-fledged advertising agency specializing in direct mail, with the unique concept that we also did all the production. Everything would be under our control, from concept to fulfillment.

But the move was terribly disruptive, and the business did not grow as quickly as anticipated. With increased overhead, we were losing between $200,000 and $300,000 a month. Add to this the wild card of inflation, too. The prime rate was near 16 percent at the time. We took a mortgage on the new building, for which we paid $13 million. We got a $10 million mortgage at 18 percent, which meant that $1.8 million a year was going to service the mortgage. And that was only the interest, not the principal.

We entered this position with full confidence in our ability to expand the business. But the element we didn't consider was the rapid and deathly increase in interest rates. We had made the commitment to buy the building the year earlier, when interest rates were much lower. To some extent, we could control the business; we had no control over interest rates.

It was a grim situation. We were one company, and the entire operation was in danger: our operation in Europe, our sales-promotion response agencies, our manufacturing facilities. We didn't know how much more we could sustain.

The straw that broke the camel's back came when my chief financial officer said, "Jack, I don't know how to tell you this, but I've had one heart attack and I don't want another. I don't know how you're going to make the payroll in January. The pressure is just too great. Because of my health, I have to resign." His health was at risk, and I accepted his resignation.

The strength of a company is not in its bricks and stones or equipment. It is in the people, and it is tested by how they respond in crisis more than how they respond in good times. Every company faces both minor and major problems, but the biggest is when the company's very existence is in danger, and the individuals behind it stand to lose everything they have worked for over the years. This is exactly what we were facing.

My partners and I got together to formulate plans that would address the situation. Harold Holland, my partner who operated Art-Mold in Providence, Rhode Island, said, "We've always produced and we're just going to make more, and manage our money better so that we can feed the funds into the corporate office. And although I'm a real nut about paying our bills, we're just going to have to make our suppliers wait so that we can get the financing we need."

His contribution was to continue to be the totally predictable company, turning out a terrific cash flow and higher profits. But he also did something that was personally painful: holding off paying debts to an extent far beyond anything he would have done had we not been facing a crisis.

Jack Nadel, Inc., under the leadership of my brother Marty, adopted the same attitude. He extended our outgoing payments, but because the company dealt in volume at a lower profit than the manufacturing company, the trick was to increase the cash flow. Marty personally became the major salesperson and the chief collector for all outstanding debts, using all the ingenuity he could muster.

We had the volume, but payment traditionally came in an average of 75 days. In those days of high interest rates, that margin had expanded to 100 days. Marty increased his sales effort, offering discounts and other incentives to get faster collection.

As far as the company's debts were concerned, Marty called on all the favors he'd given over the years, telling our chief suppliers, "Look, you are just going to have to carry me. Your normal terms are thirty days. We are going to pay you in ninety days, but we will pay you. You can count on that." And they trusted his word enough to accept that.

My associate in Europe also gave us his support. Interest rates in Europe were lower than in the United States, but on top of that, incentives made interest rates for export lower still. Our plan was to import a great deal of merchandise, sell it, and delay payment to Europe. He agreed. His job was to satisfy the European banks. By importing the merchandise, selling it, collecting, and delaying our payment to Europe, we generated a large cash flow. It's politely called "managing the money," but essentially we were delaying payment.

The greatest weight fell on the shoulders of Bob Buckingham, whose company was the one having difficulty growing into the increased overhead. Our plan in this instance was to fill the plant with work. We decided to take bulk work, the kind we normally avoided. And we would go after people who did massive mailings and offer them reduced prices. It was better to have the plant operating with a lower profit than sitting empty.

In the meantime, we resisted pressure from people who heard we were in trouble and were offering to buy into Krupp-Taylor at a reduced price. I told Bob, "I have no doubt that if we can give you enough running room, you will make Krupp-Taylor a great company." I never failed to believe that. And that's what he did. Bob went out personally and got the work to fill the plant.

My job was to refinance the building and lessen the crippling mortgage load. With the help of an excellent loan broker, I was able to engineer a deal considered very difficult at the time.

Interest rates were starting to come down, but I happened to catch an institution that needed to show a profit. I negotiated a lower interest rate, but paid a lot of points. Points are the percentage you pay an institution for processing the loan, and this money goes right to their bottom line. In normal times, you would pay one or two points, but we paid five points. In their case, five points on a $12 million loan gave them an immediate $600,000 profit. And that's what they needed to show. We refinanced the building and got an extra $2 million over the original $10 million loan, with the interest rate lowered from 18 to 15½ percent.

Our plan called for tremendous sacrifices by all the partners, but they pitched in with time and effort and made their parts work. Over the next seven months the pressure eased, and we weathered the storm. The company is many times stronger now than it was. We have made more money since 1983 than at any other time in the history of the company.

The new building for Krupp-Taylor worked out well, too. Our idea to create a full-service agency, and all the hard work that went into it, helped us acquire new clients who we would have been unable to service in the old surroundings, from both a visual and production standpoint. We didn't have the look of an agency before, but now we did and we could attract clients such as Apple, United Airlines, Marriott Hotels, and other large companies. Once the pressure eased, we grew into the new building with increased volume and profits.

In a crisis this serious, no single individual could have resolved the problems. If any part of the company had fallen apart or not delivered as magnificently as it did, Measured Marketing Services would now be history. All the people involved—my partners and their staffs—did their part.

We learned to think a little more carefully before making huge moves in the future, but we also learned that we could count on each other in a crisis, and that was probably the most valuable lesson of all.

A Most Important Partner

When choosing partners, you cannot overestimate the importance of your lifetime partner, if you have one. In my case, I've been lucky enough to have the same partner in marriage for 39 years.

My wife, Elly, had a business background before we met. She had been a model, managed a showroom, and worked as a salesperson. Thus she understood what I was doing. More important, when I decided to leave my brother's business, she showed unlimited confidence in my ability to succeed. In fact, when my brother asked me to come back, she was adamantly against it. She felt my talent would be submerged.

In 1953, after I started my first company, Elly worked
with me for the first ten years, acting as receptionist, secretary,
confidante, and executive.

It was a big decision to go out on my own, but she backed
me every step of the way. My income was terrific before I
started my own company. I made something over $20,000 in
1952, which would probably be the equivalent of $100,000
today. When I started my own business, to properly finance
it, I paid myself $100 a week and Elly $50 a week. That was
our salary for the first two years until we built up the business.
Elly's unqualified support and willingness to work hard had
more to do with my success than I can ever say. More important, over the years she has been my sounding board, my
toughest critic, and my greatest asset.

I think it very important that today's neophyte entrepreneur have the full backing of the person to whom he or she
is personally committed. It's important to have the support
of someone who can understand and communicate with you,
who can advise and act as a sounding board. Although one
doesn't normally think of it in these terms, your lifetime
partner is probably as important a business relationship as
you'll ever have.

8

Financing

As I've mentioned in the previous chapter, you make money three ways: by selling well, buying well, and running a tight ship. There's also a fourth way. A business also makes money by using the proper financing.

Financing is one of the most sophisticated and crucial areas of any business. It includes questions such as, Where should I borrow money? Where should I spend the money? Where should I buy my capital improvements? What terms should I give to purchasers? What terms should I give to sales? What are the taxes? How will interest rates affect me?—and a dozen more. Reduced to their basics these questions all have to do with getting and managing money—a phrase that could well define the concept of financing.

Financing ranges from the very basic to the very sophisticated. The better your business, the more sophisticated your management of money has to become. Everyone works to make money, but while some people manage it well, others do it badly. The difference is usually based on differing degrees of discipline and knowledge.

It's interesting how the focus on financing changes with time. The first concern of the entrepreneur is, "How much business can I do?" As he gains a little more experience, it becomes, "How much profit can I make? Volume is for ego—profit's the real thing." The third level is, "How much money can the company get to keep?" This is when he starts to worry about corporate taxes, profit sharing and pension plans, and the like. In the next level, he's concerned about how much money he can personally get, when everything else is taken care of. The final level is, "How much money can I get to keep after I've paid the government and all my personal expenses?"

Most people think of financing in the abstract until they get into business, and then it becomes very concrete. One of the first things a businessman should realize (very early in his career, when it is often overlooked) is that the cost of money should be considered part of the cost of merchandise. It's a legitimate expense.

If you borrow money, the interest charges must enter into your pricing. If you don't have to borrow, and you have a million dollars to put into your business, then you obviously don't have to pay interest on that amount. You must realize, however, that the million dollars is costing you exactly what it *would* have cost, had you borrowed it from the bank. After all, you could have invested that million dollars and made interest on it. You're not going to do that, of course, because you can make more investing it in your own business. But you *could* have made interest on it, and you have to consider that loss of interest a part of the cost of your merchandise.

I've seen many older well-established, well-financed businesses assume that the money they have doesn't cost them anything. But they could be making money on that money, simply by investing it in CDs or Treasury Bills. So why should they think it's free? It's an erroneous conclusion that gives a distorted sense of prosperity.

Most entrepreneurs and small business people do not give the whole area of financing the importance it deserves. You can hire professionals to administer this area, but you had better understand what they are doing. When you lose the money, your accountant isn't going to pay for it. And when you make it, he's not going to share in it. If the worst happened and you lost your business because you didn't understand the in's and out's of financing, you could use that as an excuse, but nobody would care. You lost it. If you find that you're backing off from the subject, the smartest thing you could do would be to take a basic course. Most people think the subject too deep, but all it takes is the discipline to learn the basics. Ignorance is no excuse.

Borrowing

I have a lifelong friend whose favorite quote is, "Neither a borrower, nor a lender be. . . . This above all: to thine own self be true." He always says he'd never borrow anything from anybody. Of course, he's a poor man today, because the world lives on credit. In fact, almost the entire population borrows these days whenever they buy merchandise on credit.

Borrowing is absolutely essential in business. It's derived from need—from what must be done to survive and expand. The key is to borrow smart, not dumb. Borrow well by knowing the nature of financing and recognizing what you are doing. By borrowing well, you can actually make money.

When we considered buying our major piece of property to house the direct-mail agency, we examined many financing alternatives. At the time, interest rates were at 18 percent and a union fund offered 10 percent financing in return for 50 percent equity in the building. Fortunately, we decided to do without the money and never gave up any of our property. We paid $13 million for the property, with original financing of $10 million at 18 percent. That meant we were paying $1.8 million in interest every year. Now we refinance that property when the prime rate goes down dramatically. When we were able to refinance at 15 percent, we did it. And we borrowed more money. The cash we got out was nontaxable. Our payments were actually less, and we got a couple of million dollars in cash from it.

Recently we refinanced at 10 percent. Keep in mind that we originally borrowed the $10 million at 18 percent and paid $1.8 million a year in interest. Now we borrowed $14 million at 10 percent, so we got $14 million in cash but our payments now are only $1.4 million a year instead of $1.8 million.

In other words, we have already borrowed all the money we originally put into the building. We got out all our cash and, essentially, we own the equity in the building for nothing.

Whether to borrow or not isn't often the question. The deal usually dictates it. But when to borrow, where to borrow, and how to borrow are very important, very individual decisions. The terms are what you are after. Eventually you are going to have to pay, but what are you going to pay with? What happens if your deal doesn't work? The real check and balance is intrinsic, however, because nobody is going to lend you money unless you have something solid to borrow on.

Sources of money today are numerous—much more so than when I was first starting out. Now banks are only one of many lenders, ranging from venture capitalists to insurance companies. There's a whole world of financing open to you. The key is to get the terms that best suit you.

All terms are negotiable. I should repeat that three times, because so many people think that they can't negotiate with a large, prestigious bank. It's not true. Everything is negotiable.

Banks base their interest rate on the prime rate. The prime is the rate set for the most solid borrowers, and theoretically everyone else borrows at something over the prime rate. If, for instance, a firm like IBM borrows money, it pays interest at the prime rate or below. If Joe Jones Computer Company borrows, depending upon its credit rating, it pays anywhere from 2 to 4 percent interest over the prime rate. As in all business, profit is directly proportional to risk. My company, because it happens to be a very good risk, borrows at an interest rate slightly less than the prime. The common belief is that no one borrows at less than the prime rate; the reality is that with a creditworthy position in the 1987 market, you could negotiate a rate below prime.

When most entrepreneurs borrow from banks they have to put up personal guarantees. That's part of the risk *they* take. It's axiomatic that banks, in order to assume as little risk as possible, take as much security as they can persuade you to give, including a lien on your firstborn son. They'll demand everything, but what you give them is a matter of negotiation. When we bought back our company, we had to put up our personal guarantees as collateral. That meant that if we were wrong, we lost everything: our homes, our cars, our children. Today, we put up zero in personal guarantees. The banks can look only to the assets of the corporation.

Financing revolves around what you're willing to give for what you expect to get. What is the potential of the deal? How much can you make and at what risk? The higher the risk, the more it's going to cost you.

If I'm worth $10 million and I want to borrow $1 million from the bank, I can do it at the lowest possible rate. But if I'm worth $1 million and I want to borrow $10 million, I'm not only going to have to pay the top rate, but I'll have to convince them there's some solid merchandise to back it up.

When you move away from bank financing, you get into things like factoring. The factor is lending you money based on your accounts receivable, and he's lending it to you at a much higher interest rate than the bank because of the greater risks involved. If you're paying a bank 10 percent interest, you may pay a factor 20 or 25 percent. Because he charges a higher interest rate, he can afford a certain percentage of loss, unlike the bank. It's a workable way to go, but keep in mind that many people who factor their invoices are making just enough money to pay the factor. You must have enough margin in your product to allow for that factoring.

The amount of money you can borrow and who you can borrow it from are directly proportional to how risky you are. If you have a strong track record, you don't have to go to a factor to finance your accounts receivable—the bank will do it. In effect, they take a lien on your accounts receivable. Instead of the accounts paying you directly, they pay the bank, and the bank gives you the difference. But it depends upon your status.

Yet another method of financing is to give away a piece of the deal, such as the alternative we had when we wanted to finance our real estate purchase. The equity position says

"We're partners. I'll put in the money and you put in the knowledge and work, and if you make it we'll split the profits." This is someone, such as a venture capitalist, who's willing to take the risk for a lion's share of the deal. Or, if you have the background credentials in business, another way to raise money is to float a public issue and get the public to invest in your project.

The letter of credit is yet another excellent financing tool, this time when doing business overseas. It states that you promise to pay when the merchandise is put on a ship or plane. It doesn't cost the bank a cent for this promise to pay—until they pay it. Meanwhile, the bank charges you a nominal fee, usually about ¾ of 1 percent to open the letter of credit. Letters of credit can be opened for as much as a year, yet all you pay is the original fee. The clock doesn't start to run on the full amount until after the bank has paid it. Then someone has to pay them for that money. But until that moment, you have nothing tied up except the initial small fee.

It all boils down to how much you want and how much you're willing to give away. Which is the best way to go? Obviously, the best way usually is where you can get the cheapest financing. If you can borrow a million dollars at 8 percent, you are $10,000 a year better off than if you borrow it at 9 percent. The difference between bank loans and factoring can be a gap of ten points, which translates to $100,000 a year—a very significant figure.

When considering how inexpensively you can finance your business, some sophisticated techniques come into the picture. Most banks make a great deal of money from medium-sized companies who do not have much in the way of financial sophistication. The best target for a bank is a company doing between $2 and $10 million a year. A company that size may have from $50,000 to $100,000 in the bank to pay their bills. And they may not know how to work the float, operate on a zero balance, or other techniques. That means their money sits there, and the bank is lending it out at interest—interest that they could be earning. Once you start dealing with large sums of money, it is imperative you either understand what you are doing or hire someone who does.

How Much?

Probably as many new businesses fail because of undercapitalization as do because of incompetence. Perhaps more. The question of how much to borrow for a business or a particular deal is of paramount importance.

Borrow as much as you really need, or even more. This is because of two reasons: If you have to go back to the well, you may lose credibility; and, worse, if you have to go back for more, you may not get it.

The first thing is to project your cash flow. Cash flow prediction is a scientific process, we are told. You can do it for every business, and every part of it is scientific, except one. There is one premise you have to guess, and that is what your gross volume is going to be.

Always allow a margin for error. I never saw a cash flow or financial projection that wasn't presented as conservative. In fact, the words invariably go together: "conservative projection." And I've also never seen a projection that has worked out conservatively. It always costs more, and you made less. Always. You have to throw in a percentage for the something you didn't anticipate, because it always shows up.

I find that if my cash flow tells me I'm going to need $1 million for the next six months, normally it is just as easy to borrow $1.4 million as $1.2 million. In fact, you don't even have to borrow it. You can get the line of credit for that amount. Then, if you need it you have it. The bank will charge you a fee to get a line of credit, but it is well worth it. If someone doesn't pay you on time, or you don't produce something in time, you have some breathing space.

Remember, however, that your financier is, in effect, your partner. You must take him into your complete confidence. With a bank, it's a formal requirement that you report back monthly to tell them that everything is happening as you planned. Bankers are nervous people; they don't like surprises. With a private financier, your procedure would be whatever the two of you agree on. It is always wise to stay in regular communication. This is not to say you should drive him crazy, but give all the pertinent information on a regular basis.

If trouble comes up, it's best to let your financier know *before* the worst happens. He might be surprisingly understanding and helpful. With bankers in particular, keep in mind that no bank wants to take over your business. If the unfortunate happens and you are close to bankruptcy, the bank will try to help you as much as possible and ride with you as long as practical rather than lose their entire investment. It depends on what they feel they can get out of it. In any event, it always pays to let your financier know what is happening, whether the news is good or bad.

Dealing with Bankers

When dealing with bankers, people think that they are involved with someone close to God, or that bankers are unbelievably brilliant people when it comes to financial matters. The fact is that there are as many stupid bankers as there are stupid dentists or stupid businessmen. When we moved our company from Italy to France, after losing a great deal of money, we needed French financing. We did it there through the American Express bank. Unfortunately, my chief financial officer at the time and the manager of the French company had come up with some very optimistic projections which, of course, they had called "conservative." Thus, we ran out of cash and had to come up with an entirely new financial package to refinance.

I went to the Paris office of the bank and met with a very haughty and condescending French banker. He laughed at me. "You crazy Americans," he said. "You come over here to do business and your people's projections are all wrong. This is ridiculous!"

"Wait a minute," I said. "First of all, I'm chairman of the company, and I don't like to hear my people spoken of that way. Second, I don't care what your opinion is. If you don't want to refinance, I'll go somewhere else."

At first he was shocked, but then he put on his best patronizing air. He persisted in being stupid. I withdrew from that bank and took our business elsewhere.

I came on strong because I had nothing to lose. Some bankers, because they have money that you want, abuse their power. Never let them hoodwink or overpower you. Keep in mind that there are many banks in competition with each other. And most of them want your business. Do your homework in dealing with bankers, just as you do in every other phase of business. Know your banker's position within the bank, how much authority he has, how big a commitment he can make before going to the committee, how strong his position is within the committee, and how well he'll make a presentation for you.

Usually the loan officer has an officer above him who supervises a group of loan officers. Then there's a committee who supervises the supervisor. The loan departments are divided according to category: real estate, business, entertainment, and so on. The head man for all these groups is usually a vice president and officer of the bank. Each time you increase your level of borrowing, you move up a step in the approval ladder.

It makes sense to meet everyone involved, so that the person can match a face to a request that is otherwise faceless. If it is necessary to go over someone's head, it makes a big difference if you are known when you call. Also, in big banks the loan officers change with great regularity. It pays to know the top man because he's more constant. Additionally, there may be times you find you just can't relate to your loan officer. He or she doesn't understand what you are doing and won't or can't work with you. It is perfectly within your province (and most people aren't aware of this) to call his superior and request a new loan officer. Yet another reason you should know the top people is that sometimes you have an emergency that requires large sums to be transferred quickly. Often, this is beyond the authority of the loan officer, but you can call the person above him and get it accomplished fast.

I don't believe in wining and dining bankers or "having a close personal relationship" with my banker, but it does pay to let them know who you are and to keep in touch regularly. As in any other phase of business, communication is important. As I said earlier, bankers hate surprises. If anything is going to change, let them know before someone else does.

Everything you do is a sales job in one form or another. Banking is no exception. If you're requesting a bank loan, you have to touch the banker's "hot" button. And that happens to be security. The bank is in business for only one thing: to buy and sell money. Because of the small margin between buying and selling, they have to make sure they aren't taking a chance. If you can convince them (a) that you're honest and resourceful, (b) that you have a track record of meeting all your commitments, and (c) that your business is fully capable of servicing the debt, a lot of other things can pass by the boards. Never ask a banker to take an extraordinary position. He won't. Show him how safe the deal is, and he'll be happy to help. If you can't communicate with one banker, find another you can communicate with. He will prove to be a valuable and helpful ally.

How Financing Affects Your Business

Financing is a major factor to consider when handling your daily business affairs. Interest rates and the overall cost of money should form integral parts of every deal you make.

For example, in buying merchandise, let's say you have trade terms that offer you a 2 percent discount if you pay within ten days. When the prime rate is at 8 percent, that's a good deal. If you are paying two points over prime for your money, or let's say 10 percent, you are paying less than 1 percent a month. And if you get 2 percent off, you are, in effect, making 1 percent on it. But let's reverse that and assume that the prime is at 16 percent and you are paying 20 percent. In that case, you are paying almost 2 percent per month for your money, and the discount offers you no advantage.

Not only should you look at what money is costing you, but you should also be aware of what it is costing the person you are doing business with. If you are buying from a company that offers you 90 days' credit, it has to pay interest on the money it uses for that period. If you have a great deal of cash and the quality of the merchandise is not a concern, you can negotiate to pay 90¢ per unit instead of $1 if you offer to pre-pay the invoice. The benefit to the other party is that he doesn't have to worry about financing the amount for the 90-day period.

You have to qualify your supplier's finances, as well as his work. Who is he? Is he short on cash or long? How important to him is immediate payment? If I deal with a badly financed pure maker of a product—"pure" meaning one who only manufactures to order and does not market, sell, or even plan production goals for what he makes—and I give him a custom job, he will often say, "But I can't afford to buy the material." It's an opportunity to negotiate a better price. Sometimes, you can offer to pay for the material or perhaps offer 50 percent payment with the order and the balance on delivery. It all depends upon what works for both of you.

Financing affects everything, including your inventory. If interest rates are low and stable, inflation is low and stable because the two go hand-in-hand. In that case, you have less tendency to stock up on real merchandise because prices are not going to rise in the immediate future. But if inflation is rising, it's a different story. You're going to buy more inventory. If you pay $20 for a radio today, you can just hold it and sell it a year from now for $30. In countries such as Israel, where interest rates were astronomical and prices went up daily, you didn't want to sell anything. The longer you held merchandise, the more money you got for it.

Interest rates dictate many of your business practices, such as what terms you give purchasers. If interest rates are low, you don't have to offer unusual incentives to get people to pay quickly. If interest rates are high, you have to chase that money very hard. Likewise, if rates are low, you don't save much by holding your accounts payable, and you're better off keeping a good trade relationship. If the interest rates are high, then you have an incentive not to pay your bills until you have to.

When getting into import and export, and considering overseas financing, you'll find substantially the same situation, with some slight variations. Right now, you can borrow in Switzerland at 5 percent, in the United States at 8 percent, and in France at about 11 percent. This makes a difference as to where you put your business. Where do you want to finance it? Where do you want the main organization? Where do you want your profits to fall? Because of our new tax law, people are going to want to put their profits in the United States rather than elsewhere. Our maximum tax of 28 percent is considerably lower than anywhere else in the world.

Because of financing, it is sometimes wise to consider establishing a company overseas. If a country is keen on encouraging export, which most of them are, there are incentives. Most countries (except the United States) offer favorable loan rates for export shipments. If the normal borrowing rate in France is 11 percent, you can probably borrow at 9 percent to export French merchandise.

In France, West Germany, Italy, Switzerland, and other European countries, you can borrow against export shipments. After the shipment, you can take the documents to the bank and they will lend you the full amount of the invoice, at a very good rate. To get the same accommodation in the United States, you have to go to a factor, who factors your accounts receivable for as much as double what a bank would charge. An overseas bank, however, will finance you at less than the normal domestic rate, as long as it's an export shipment. In Japan, for example, the accommodation is so great that a company such as Sony can ship to its own warehouse in New York and get that shipment fully financed at export rates.

The buzzword of all these countries is *export*. Say the word and doors open. You get preferential treatment in taxes, locations, and other incentives. The other buzzword is *jobs*. Use the key words *export* and *jobs*, and incentives flow your way. Except in the United States. This is a ridiculous state of affairs, considering the problems we are having with our balance of trade and our necessity to increase exports. In the United States, if you want to increase your business and expand overseas, you need collateral to get the money. The more business you do, the more orders you book, the more financing you need—and the more difficult it becomes to get it, even though you have the business. In Europe and most countries in the Orient, the moment you take that shipping document to the bank, the financing doors open and capital is easily acquired.

Financing in the international arena is no more difficult than in the domestic—only slightly more complex. And, happily, the complexity enters only because your options have increased. If you are a good businessman domestically and get good financing advice in that arena, you should have no trouble extending that same expertise beyond the borders of the United States.

Help

One of the wisest investments any growing company can make is to get the best financial help possible. Don't ever buy cheap financial help. Of course, if you don't have large holdings and you are not into heavy financing, you don't need Joe DiMaggio at the plate. But get the best help you can afford.

Particularly when it comes to taxes, the financial field is so specialized now that it really pays to have someone who knows his business. He will not only make your life a great deal easier, but he can point out avenues to deals you never thought you could handle. Entrepreneurs are not well known for their attention to details. It's easier to have someone who is detail-conscious do it for you, so you can do what you do best.

Take the trouble to carefully check out your financial advisor, as you would any other business associate. I took great care in choosing my chief financial officer and my tax lawyer, and it has paid off a hundredfold. Don't succumb to the temptation of hiring someone cheaply, who will learn these sophisticated tasks on the job. You don't want job trainees handling something as important as your finances. Good financial help is the cheapest thing you can buy.

9

Workable Marketing

Marketing is a small word that covers a large area. It embraces all the activities involved in getting a product from seller to buyer: sales, advertising, distribution, shipping, and anything else you have to do to put that item in the hands of a buyer. It could be defined as the act of deciding upon the proper marketplace for your product, of choosing the best possible way to present that product, and of determining how best to distribute the product. Those are the basic elements.

The diverse skills needed to market a product successfully involve creativity, imagination, a flair for showmanship, pragmatism, organizational ability, persistence, financial acumen, and—of course—luck. Business school graduates with advanced degrees like to think of marketing as a science. They can cite a score of inviolate axioms and principles. But there's more than a little art involved—and maybe even some magic. In spite of academics and theorists, marketing actually has few hard-and-fast rules. Marketing techniques vary widely according to product.

To come up with a workable marketing plan, however, there are some standard questions that must be asked. Who can use the product? What is the life of the product? Are you equipped to supply that marketplace? If not, is the product strong enough for you to get equipped, or should you find someone else already in place? In other words, every product has to be examined on its own merits as well as on the basis of your own capabilities. Is it worth it? And what will it take to bring it to market?

There is only one marketing rule to remember: *There is no such thing as a foolproof marketing scheme.* Major companies, with virtually unlimited marketing resources, have proved this point over and over. The hundreds of millions of dollars Ford put behind its Edsel car came to naught. I.B.M., one of the greatest companies in the world, put millions of dollars into researching and marketing its first personal computer—and had to withdraw it from the market. You'd think that a unique service like trans-Atlantic Concorde flights would be a marvelous success. (Less than four hours to fly from London or Paris to New York!) It has been an unbelievably costly proposition, and it has never been successful. Why? Something was missing in the marketing mix. What? I don't have the answer. There are certain mysteries to that mix which defy explanation.

It always comes down to a few truisms. In marketing a product, you must know the product: where it can be sold, how you can get it there, and how big the marketplace is. The failures are usually found within these parameters. Perhaps there is only a limited marketplace for the Concorde— one not being enough to withstand the enormous research and development costs that went into it. Unfortunately, we'll never know how much those costs were because the plane was developed by a government consortium, which has the power to bury the figures.

As a kind of last word on this, the advertising specialty industry started an annual practice of choosing the "New Product of the Year." It became a joke within the industry because for ten successive years, not one of those products was ever successful in the marketplace. There's no such thing as a foolproof marketing scheme.

Oops!

Believe it or not, I've made mistakes myself. As I said earlier, I have a whole warehouse full of them. Even as recently as

1984, after many years of business experience, I made a major marketing error.

We owned the licence for the Pierre Cardin trademark in two categories of products: stationery and writing instruments; and electronic products such as radios, television sets, calculators, telephones, and so on. In 1984, we licensed an American electronics company to manufacture Pierre Cardin products to be sold around the world. But we made one major mistake. We told the manufacturer that we wanted him to distribute his electronics products through the same network of distributors we had for our writing instruments and stationery.

It didn't seem like a mistake at the time. Why not use the distribution that was already established? The distributors are already selling Pierre Cardin consumer products, and the electronics items are consumer products. Logically they should go to the same consumer outlets.

Wrong. We didn't really examine the nuances of the electronics business. In writing instruments there are traditional lines of distribution, and most of the products are what we call "blind" items, meaning that there is no way really to assess the value except through the value that has already been established. For example, there is a wild pricing variation among pens such as Cross, Parker, Sheaffer, and a non-name brand. The difference in manufacturing cost is minimal, yet there may be one pen selling for 20 times the price of the same pen with the same material. The difference between the best ink in a pen and the worst is 2¢. So, although there is little variation in cost, there is great variation in pricing. It's the same with an item like perfume; the difference is only in the packaging. And it's the advertising put behind the product that determines the price.

Electronics presents an entirely different situation. The margins are much smaller, and the market is much wider. It's a discount business. You don't usually find a Cross or a Parker pen in the cheapest discount store, but you will find a Panasonic, a Sony, or a Zenith product. That's the nature of the distribution.

Electronics distributors around the world are geared to heavy volume and small markups. Pen distributors are geared to a relatively small market and a large markup. If you want to buy a radio in Paris, you go to a discount store. You do the same in Los Angeles or Tokyo. You'll find that radio in places where they sell tonnage, not in fashionable department stores.

We did our electronics products licensee a great disservice by forcing it into the same distribution outlets as our other products. It didn't work. Even though it was a consumer item and went under the same brand name, it just didn't work. Writing instruments is an item business; electronics is a tonnage business. The two don't mix.

We rectified our error, of course. But it was a costly and time-consuming marketing mistake. In marketing, you have to know that each product has a different set of standards and must be looked at individually. We learned the hard way never to distribute radios through writing instrument outlets. Never go against the grain. It's a rule we've known for a long time. At times we have chosen to break it and have gotten away with it. This time we didn't get away with it, and had to pay the price.

Go With the Flow

Always take the path of least resistance, for the simple reason that you will reach your goal quicker. Re-educating the public is a long, hard, and expensive chore.

For instance, we're in the direct-mail business, but we don't try to convert people to that method of advertising. We don't try to tell heavy users of newspaper and television advertising why direct mail is better for them. If we did, we would first have to sell them on direct mail, then sell ourselves as the best company to do the job. Rather, we go to people who must be in the mail all the time. These are the real prospects. We don't try to create a prospect that doesn't exist, because we know it's not within the capabilities of 99 percent of the companies in the world to create their own market, and we're one of that majority.

In marketing as in business generally, it is usually best to go with the flow. I've seen Americans disrupt the whole pace of a French restaurant. The French are used to a leisurely routine. First comes the soup, then the main course, the salad, the dessert, and finally the coffee. If an American comes in and says, "I want coffee first," or "I want salad before soup," it throws the rhythm off.

You can't disturb the rhythm when overseas. In Japan, if they want to serve you tea before getting down to brass tacks and they ask you to take your shoes off before entering the room, you do it. If you are a Scotch drinker and you are taken to a Japanese geisha parlor where sake is served, drink the sake. Don't ask for margaritas in Germany; you're not going to get anything that's remotely drinkable. It's the same in business. When negotiating and when marketing, observe the standards and habits of the country.

When marketing, however, if the stakes are big enough, the need is strong enough, and you have the resources, it is sometimes worth trying to change the normal patterns. But you had better know what you're taking on. Changing habits can be very difficult when it comes to people, companies, and countries.

International Marketing

In the context of international trade, marketing is concerned with two things: how to bring products that have proved successful on domestic markets into the foreign marketplace; and how to bring successful foreign products to the United States. Let's examine both, starting with the exports.

The first rule of exporting is to choose only a product that has been successful in the United States. Earlier, we said that a good product is a good product any place in the world,

and a bad product is a bad product anywhere. So if you have
the idea that you're going to dispose of a dog item in some
faraway overseas market, forget it. The best thing to do with
a real dog is to dispose of it at a fraction of your cost with
a ten-cent sale; or drop it in the ocean, bury it, or burn it,
because the longer you carry it and the more you worry about
it, the worse it becomes.

If you are a domestic manufacturer or distributor and you
have a successful product with a great history, then marketing
it in a foreign country becomes a piece of cake. You know
it's going to succeed, and you know what kind of audience to
sell it to. It's like watching a horse race, then betting on it;
it's difficult to lose.

There are certain qualifications, however. Generally you
can't take a modern product into an underdeveloped country,
and you can't bring an ordinary product into a highly competitive market without an edge. But you must start with the
advantage of taking your product or service into a country
with a standard of living and technology similar to your own.

An almost classic example was the way we took our
specialty advertising business into Europe 12 years ago. We
chose to go against the grain, but we had the resources to
pull it off.

The specialty advertising industry in the United States
is well established and organized. As I've described earlier in
this book, our complex of companies manufactured products
that were imprinted and sold through a network of distributors
to companies who used these products as promotional and
advertising giveaways. Simply put, the industry works as follows: One group of companies is the manufacturers and the
other, distributors. The distributor has a sales force that sells
to the end user, who then gives the merchandise away as an
advertising piece. The manufacturer drop-ships directly to the
customer and invoices the distributor. When he places the
order with the manufacturer, the distributor supplies his own
labels so that the customer seemingly receives the product
from the distributor, even though it was shipped by the manufacturer. After the distributor receives his invoice showing

that the product was shipped, he invoices it to his customer. And that's the end of the circle. Very orderly.

When I investigated the specialty advertising business in Europe, I found a much more fragmented industry. I also found that the products, the sales techniques, and the methods of distribution were about ten years behind the United States.

In France, I visited the most prominent people in the business and found their entire product lines and procedures antiquated. There were no computers or automatic setting machines in the imprinting process, for example; it was all done by hand. The items were hand-screened or hand-stamped, the typesetting was elementary, and those that had them used old-fashioned brass dies. The results of all this quite primitive activity were poorly printed products with poor graphics—all in all, a quality well below what we were capable of and products that turned out more expensive than we could provide.

Because the industry wasn't organized in Europe, distributors searched the market, found manufactured products suitable for giveaways, brought them to their own warehouses, imprinted them (badly) to order, then shipped them to their customers. It was a market ripe for entry.

We decided on France because they had a very active specialty industry and had already accepted the idea of specialty advertising. You didn't have to sell them on it.

We had an established line of low-cost specialties that had proved successful in the United States. Our marketing problem in France was to identify the distributors, introduce them to our product line, show them how we successfully sold the product, and then, most of all, give them our distribution technique.

That was the essential marketing problem: to introduce a new concept of distribution. It was going against the grain, but it would make life easier for them. They would no longer have to inventory the merchandise, which eliminated a big cost factor. By letting us imprint, they would get that problem out of their hair, too, and receive a much better product. In the U.S. system, the distributor sells and doesn't handle; it is far more efficient and cost-effective. In France, the distributor didn't just handle paper; he controlled all facets of the merchandise. If he found merchandise in the south of France, he would have it shipped to his warehouse in Paris, imprint it, then, perhaps, ship it back to a customer in the south of France. Our system eliminated all those handling costs and freight charges, and resulted in a superior product. Once the French accepted our distribution method, we felt the rest would be relatively easy. Not only were the products superior, but we had successful techniques to sell them.

Behind all advertising and marketing is the realization that you must ultimately prove yourself. Your customer has to be better off than he was before you came on the scene. I have never liked saying to a prospective customer, "I would like to replace your present supplier." I would much rather say, "I will give you something that no one has ever given you before, and help you increase your business."

That's a workable rule around the corner and around the world. If I can show how, through my products, my processes, my techniques, and my service, I can help a client increase his business, then I'm going to have a customer. If, ultimately, I don't prove that, I have nothing.

Our biggest problem, it turned out, was convincing the distributors that they could trust us. This wasn't easy to do anywhere in Europe, but was particularly difficult in France, where nobody trusts anybody. We had to convince the distributors that they could send their orders to us identifying their customers, and we would ship directly to the customers under their labels and never invoice the customers directly or deal directly with the customers. In other words, we had to prove we wouldn't steal their customers.

The reactions ranged from skepticism to hostility. Here were a bunch of cocky Americans not only saying that Europeans were behind the times, but promising to show them how to expand their businesses. It's interesting to note that while most American businessmen are optimistic, European businessmen tend to be skeptical of everything, including optimism.

We realized that we couldn't change ingrained attitudes overnight. It wouldn't work to launch a huge advertising campaign saying, "Look guys, we're honest people and you can trust us to ship to your customers without selling directly to them." What we did instead was hold seminars for the distributors' sales forces in which essentially we said, "I have a promotion that worked. I'm going to bring it to you intact and show you how you can make it work for you." The seminars introduced the product and showed them how and where to sell. In some cases, we actually accompanied the salesmen on their personal calls to help them sell.

The changes didn't happen quickly. It was a gradual process and took several years. But it was inevitable. The idea was right, the product line was good, the sales approach was proper. If you picked one or two of the leading distributors in an area and successfully put your merchandising into those companies—and they succeeded with it—suddenly you had a forward-looking, aggressive distributor who was competing in the field with our modern-designed and beautifully imprinted products. It's just a matter of time before the others said, "Hey, I'd like to have that, too."

The trust factor took time, too. The toughest part was proving that we would adhere to the rules we had established. We had to prove our veracity, credibility, and honor. If occasionally an end customer found us and asked for a quote on a particular product he had seen elsewhere, we would refuse. "We only quote through Pierre Gaston, who originally sold the product," we would say. "They are the distributor; please contact them." Instead of just letting it drop there, we also contacted Pierre Gaston to make sure he knew we had referred a customer to him. Gradually, people realized we really did carry through on what we promised.

Changing habits is a costly affair. Every so often, there is an opportunity to make a breakthrough in a marketplace, but be prepared to sustain some losses while you are doing it. Before we succeeded in France we were in debt for a couple of million dollars.

When we first entered the French market, people told us it couldn't be done. "They'll never change the system." "They don't trust each other, they'll never trust you." But the successful pattern of product line and distribution had worked in the United States, and it was brought to Europe as a total package.

The French industry changed because of our presence there. For example, we found that if a company only had six sales people, it didn't pay to stage a seminar. In those cases we rented a hotel meeting room and invited all the distributors in the area to come with their salespeople. We were told, "That's impossible. I wouldn't be seen in the same room with that turkey." But we did it. The first seminars were sparsely attended; now when we hold one of these seminars in Paris, for instance, the room is full. Over the years the distributors learned that they wouldn't lose their competitive edge if they talked to each other. In fact, they found that if they compared notes about processing, handling orders, and other business elements, they actually could increase their business. This is what trade associations do, of course. But in this industry the participants were totally antagonistic to each other until we became the catalyst.

Twelve years have passed, and today our company dominates the specialty advertising business in France. I think our presence there has elevated the entire industry. They have better merchandise at a better price, better salespeople, and better communication with each other. It has been a good deal for everyone, even though we went against the grain to do it.

Bringing It Back Home

The other side of the international trade coin is bringing products to the United States that have proved successful overseas. About seven or eight years ago I attended the specialty trade show in Düsseldorf and became friendly with an importer who was the largest supplier of luggage items in West

Germany. These were the light carry-on type luggage, as opposed to heavy luggage.

He was showing a unique bag at his booth. It was an expandable tote bag that collapsed into itself. It folded into a very small size, but when unzipped, it became a full-size carrying bag. It was a tremendous item. It had a thousand uses, from a beachwear item to extra luggage for travelers who wanted a bag in which to bring back additional items.

I noticed that the bag was imported from Hong Kong, which posed a problem. "This is a sensational product," I told him, "but if you import it from Hong Kong and I import it from you in Germany, it's going to make the price too high."

He agreed and posed a solution. "Tell you what I'll do," he said. "I'll give you my source of supply in Hong Kong. I'll act as your agent and take a 5 percent commission on it. You open your letter of credit directly to the factory in Hong Kong." It was a deal. It would have cost me money and time to find the product myself. Now was the time to strike, because this was a hot item and would be all over the place in short order.

Based on experience, I knew the item would be hot and I didn't need a comprehensive market study. There was no doubt in my mind that it would be a popular item. You always look for this type of product, but find it all too seldom. This is one of the tremendous advantages, however, of being in the international marketplace. I would never have discovered it if I hadn't been in West Germany.

I packed half a dozen samples in my bag and brought them home to present to my sales force. They all flipped over it, so we sent a telex to the supplier in Hong Kong (who had already been contacted by my German friend) and ordered a sample shipment of 200 bags to be sent by air. Ten days later we had the bags and the salesmen went out with them. The bags took off like a shot. We sold them strictly as premium or specialty items. Sometimes they were imprinted with a name or given as business gifts; others were used as traffic-building premiums.

We did a great deal of business with the expandable bag, and it's still a stable item. However, we sold it in great quantities in the first year because we were first in the market; by the second year, it had lost its luster. Too many people got into the market. Today, we don't import it, but buy it from local importers.

The fact that this was a hot, yet generic, item dictated our marketing strategy. We had no particular edge except that we could be first with it in the market and our distribution was already in place. We couldn't make it any better, buy it any cheaper, or import it any faster than anyone else. We knew that once the bag proved successful there would be hundreds of importers who would bring it in. When that happened, the market would become extraordinarily competitive. If, for instance, the item cost $2 and I could sell if for $4, in a year someone would be buying it for the same price and selling it for only $2.25. At that point there's no room in the market anymore. With an item like this, you get in fast, make your profit, and get out.

Remember the three categories of products I mentioned in Chapter 5: standard, hot, and trademark merchandise. Each category demands a different marketing strategy. The tote bag was in the second category—a hot item. When you have an agreement with someone to bring in an item which has a patent or trademark, you have limited exclusivity, putting the item into the first category. With items in this group your marketing strategy is more long range. The third group of products includes items you control with your own trademark, such as our line of Pierre Cardin items. Anyone could make a pen like ours, but he can't use the same name.

If possible, always go for exclusivity, but bear in mind that it's a two-edged sword. If you import, you want an exclusive. If you export, you want to sell to everybody because, frankly, exclusivity doesn't always work. If you sell to two people in the same town, you expand the market. If you sell to six people, you don't multiply it by six, but you might get twice as much business. Even though the first distributor may be unhappy about the competition, he'll work harder to sell the product. If you go by my theory that a deal should be good for everyone, don't take an exclusive product unless you know you can do a really good job with it.

It would have been silly for me to put a lot of effort into expanding the marketplace for the tote bag. No matter how good I am, I'm going to lose the market eventually. Too many other people can get into it. As long as I'm not willing to sell something at its lowest price, I'm going to lose the market on that kind of general product.

The first category, however, demands some marketing effort with a finite life. Even though the product has a name or patent with an aura of exclusivity, you are likely to lose it after a period of time, simply because of the nature of business. Perhaps the manufacturer will give it to someone else to expand his marketplace. Perhaps you don't perform as well as promised and he takes it away from you. In many cases, you won't even start out with exclusive distribution rights, but join the crowd because it's a good product and you can make a fair profit on it.

The third category, products for which you own the trademark, is where you put your strongest marketing effort. Pull out all the advertising, promotion, and sales stops because you are not only looking at today or tommorrow or next year, but at ten years down the road, too.

We are in the process of designing a new writing instrument under the Pierre Cardin name. It's ours, from concept to execution. I want to get the widest possible distribution network that I can, and I am going to seek the longest life I can possibly get for it. I'm not looking for a novelty item. I told the designer I wanted a classic—something that was going to last for a long time. It will be modern, made of today's materials, but unique and enduring and in no way trendy. Obviously, my marketing efforts for this product or line of products will be entirely different from what they were for the tote bag.

Our world distribution network has to be ready. I'm going to take it into the retail marketplace, so we have to plan an advertising campaign. I'm doing direct marketing as well as everything else I possibly can. Because this is my unique product and I want it to have a long life, I am willing to put time, effort, and money into preparing the marketplace for its arrival.

Products must be judged on their merits, and they demand different marketing strategies. My German friend's strategy with the tote bag was to import directly into West Germany and serve the market there. When opportunity presented itself, however, he found an auxiliary market in the United States by acting as a broker.

Two factors entered my marketing of the product. After determining that the product was successful in West Germany and making the judgment that it would be equally so in the United States, I had to find the lowest price source. I followed one of the main rules of trade: not to get hung up on communications or delivery. The shortest distance between two points is a straight line. I could never have economically imported the bag from Düsseldorf because it was being imported from Hong Kong.

The second factor was timing. I had to look at the life of the product. I quickly saw that it would become abundant within a year. Although I have a network of distributors, I also have a direct sales force. I had no time to set up a complex chain. The best I could do was give it to my direct sales force and have them sell it directly to their customers. And that's exactly what I did. Assess the product, assess your capabilities, and then act accordingly.

Marketing cannot succeed when you follow rules by rote. It takes imagination, adaptability, and more than a little chutzpah. While you keep one foot firmly planted on the ground, you should be prepared to reach out to higher and more intuitive levels.

Timing

People will tell you that timing is everything. Perhaps that is overstating the matter, but in marketing, timing is extraordinarily important. Major companies have gone down the tubes because they didn't pay attention to timing. The old Penn Central comes to mind. It stayed in the railroad business, sitting with a dead technology, until it folded. It should have moved into the transportation business and expanded its marketplace. The great steel companies were perfect for their time, then they hit their peak and began a downward slide. Timing dictates when to change or expand a business, when to enter a market and when to leave it, when to import and when to export.

Time is relative. It distorts, changes, converts situations, and every businessman should be aware of it. Many companies have died because they said, "It was good enough before, so it's good enough now." Well, it isn't. Markets will accept only certain products at certain times.

In the 1950s the market accepted *Father Knows Best* and *Gidget*. In the 1960s, flower children were the rage, and you could sell anything with a peace symbol. The 1980s are a different time zone. You can find case after case of items, processes, and concepts that were good in one time zone, only to become extinct in the next. And with today's speedy communications, the switch in time zones can come as quickly as a matter of months.

To protect yourself, be aware of everything that goes on around you. Ostriches can't see much when their heads are in the sand. Today, there is a merchandising revolution taking place. You can see it in the success of specialty retail outlets and with home shopping on cable television. New technology is proliferating at an incredible pace, and markets are changing faster than ever. You can't operate with invisible blinders that stop you from seeing what is happening.

International trade is more necessary than ever, if only because of timing. Technology in Japan and West Germany dramatically affects consumption in the United States. The timing is right for American businessmen to insert themselves into the world marketplace to stay on top of the changes that are taking place elsewhere.

When we exported pens to Europe when no one else was doing it, we succeeded because of our timing. The environment had changed. Owing to a shift in currency values, prosperous conditions in Europe had raised wages; our technological expertise allowed us to compete and export efficiently.

If you investigated exporting a product or process in 1984 and found you couldn't compete, it's very likely that you could have a huge market for that same product in 1988. Why are you competitive in 1988 and not in 1984? Timing.

Some people feel that timing is a matter of luck. Generally, however, it is based on knowledge—knowledge of technology, of the marketplace, of your own capabilities. The right marketing of the wrong product doesn't work, no matter how ingenious you are. The same goes for the wrong marketing of the right product. It takes the right product and the right marketing to create the right time. It's the difference between success and failure.

10

The Strength of Distribution

One of the most vital and powerful parts of the product mix is distribution. The factor that controls distribution controls almost everything. And the company that doesn't control distribution is most vulnerable.

There are a hundred different ways to distribute merchandise, ranging from selling to an importer to selling directly to the consumer. The method is dictated by the product, the consumer target for the product, the margins, and your own capabilities. The decision on how to distribute is a mix of factors: about 50 percent is determined by the product itself, 25 percent is determined by the marketplace and the margins, and 25 percent comes from your own gut feelings.

Theoretically, the more direct your distribution, the better off you are. If you sold directly to the customer—rather than to the importer, who sells to distributors, who sell to stores, who sell to customers—you'd think your margins would be better. This is not necessarily true. If you assume any of these different functions, then you take the markups that go with them. Advertisements that claim merchandise is direct from the factory to the consumer misrepresent the situation. There are costs for distribution, and they are borne by either the distributor or the manufacturer. The only difference is that the distributor is definitely going to take a profit. The question is, will you take a profit for that phase of business if you perform that function?

For a business to be viable, there must be fair profits on all ends. In the United States, our company is both manufacturer and distributor. You could say that because we manufacture in Providence and distribute in Los Angeles, we could eliminate one profit and benefit the customer. But ultimately that is a bad way to go. If you perform a function, you have to make a profit on that function, or it becomes a dead weight on other divisions in the company. It takes money to set up and distribute, just as it does to manufacture.

This is not profit for profit's sake. Each phase must have a definite function in the marketplace. Indeed, business takes a turn for the worse when people tack on profits for services or functions that are not being performed. For example, if I introduce you to a potential customer, I ask for a commission on all your business with that customer. Then, at that point, I step out. I don't service the customer in any way, and I perform no further function. I'm really getting a finder's fee. But if I stretch that into a continuing commission, then I'm taking money out of the mix, and eventually it will make you noncompetitive. If, instead, I take a one-time finder's fee, my function benefits everyone, and I'm not crippling your competitive capabilities.

Unfortunately, this mutually beneficial approach is not always the case owing to the greed of finders and the less-than-sanguine approach of the man actually doing the selling. There is a legitimate place in the market for finders, such as business brokers involved in acquisitions. They serve as matchmakers between buyers and sellers. But can you imagine what would happen if the business broker demanded a continuous fee from all business that ensued from that point on? It would be a ridiculous situation.

The Middle Eastern oil business is an excellent example of this practice carried to an extreme. It's an economy based on a great deal of corruption. "I'll introduce you to this sheik, but I want 5 percent of everything you do from now on." This worked to some degree when oil cost $30 a barrel, but at $10 a barrel (and even later, at $18 a barrel) it became a yoke around business's neck and couldn't be sustained.

In seeking distribution, I want people who give continuing service. If I sell to an importer, he is always searching his market for customers, doing the financing, and delivering to his customers Freight on Board (FOB) his plant or his warehouse. He is serving a function. If I sell to a stocking jobber, he is going to make an investment, insert my merchandise into his range, stock it in his warehouse, put it in his catalog, equip his salesmen with it, and take it out into the marketplace. These are all imperative functions, whether he does them or I do them myself.

Types of Distribution

Distribution costs money and affects margins. Choosing among the many alternatives is dictated by the type of item, the margins and the marketplace. Let's look at the various forms, from the least expensive to the most.

The first approach is to use a broker. A broker is exactly what the name implies. He has no inventory and takes no risk. He sells or buys for you and makes a commission on the transaction. Keeping in mind the risk:profit ratio, brokers represent the lowest margin that has to be sustained in the chain.

The second approach involves using an importer. An importer buys from you and may or may not sell the product before he buys it, but he is still taking all the risks of business. If anything goes wrong between the time he contracts for the merchandise and sells it to his customers—be they distributors, jobbers, or consumers—he is taking the risks of business. His markup is therefore going to be much higher. The price of the product when it lands in the foreign country is going to be higher than if you deal through a broker, but the importer eliminates your risk and guarantees distribution.

The third approach is even more direct. You bypass the importer and call on the distributor or jobber in the foreign country. In essence, you've become your own importer and you deliver directly to the distributors. This is what I did in France, and is what I do in the United States.

The fourth approach is to eliminate the broker, importer, and distributor, and sell directly to the trade. This is what most name brands do; they become their own distributors.

Companies evolve through these stages. Look at companies such as Sony or Panasonic. When they entered the U.S. marketplace, they dealt with U.S. importers who handled radios. But as their fame and distribution grew, they left the importers and went to exclusive distributors. When the marketplace grew even larger, they moved to the final stage and eliminated the distributors. Now they do the whole job themselves. This is why manufacturer's representatives have a common complaint: "The better job we do, the quicker we sell ourselves out of a job." Once they've given the distribution to the manufacturer, the manufacturer doesn't need them; he puts in his own sales force.

The product dictates distribution. Don't make the mistake we made a few years ago and distribute radios through pen distributors. They don't know what the hell to do with them. What is the product? What is the market? What markups can the product sustain? It's like pricing a product. Do you take a small markup and go for large volume, or do you take a larger markup and go for smaller volume?

In distribution you have to look at what you can sustain. If my production is limited and I want to export to 50 countries, the simplest thing is to sell to importers in those countries. There's no way I can create vast demand and satisfy the marketplace. On the other hand, if I'm I.B.M., with enormous resources and a vast potential market, I can't depend on anyone else to do my marketing job. I become my own manufacturer, importer, distributor, and sales force.

Entrepreneurs don't have the resources of giant multinational corporations, of course. Individuals who bring products to the marketplace certainly don't have comparable facilities, marketing muscle, or financing. They have to find the shortest, fastest means of distribution. As they improve their position, they can start moving through the distribution alternatives.

Sony is a household name today, but how it became that way is an interesting story. In one of its first attempts to distribute in the United States, it approached Bulova. Bulova liked the product and wanted Sony to manufacture exclusively under the Bulova name. The company used the argument that it took 50 years to create the Bulova name, and it would sell more radios as Bulova than as Sony.

Mr. Akio Morita, president of Sony, turned down the easy sale. He knew that in the long term, it would be best to have a label of his own—one that people would learn to trust and want to buy. Today, of course, people don't go in a store to buy a radio; they ask for a Sony. Forty years or so later, the Bulova name is almost extinct, while Sony is world renowned.

Soon after he turned down Bulova, Mr. Morita went with the first transistor radios to a chain of stores that loved the product and asked for quotations on quantities from 5,000 to 100,000 radios. He realized that the company would have to stretch its capacity to fulfill an order for 100,000 radios, and other markets would suffer. Perhaps it was tempting on a short-term basis, but what of the future? What would happen next year?

What did Morita do? He quoted the buyer prices as following: The highest per unit price was for 100,000; 50,000 was a little lower; 25,000 was lower yet. His best price was for a 10,000-unit order—better than for 5,000 units.

The buyer thought he was crazy, but wound up buying 10,000 units, which is exactly what Morita wanted. Sony's president didn't do the obvious and go for the quick and easy buck. Instead, he went for distribution that would give his product life, would not put all his eggs in one basket, and that would allow him to build production properly. Now that is distribution—thinking distribution.

Keeping Control

You can find people to make things, to engineer products, to administer finances, but if you don't have the distribution, you have nothing. If you have distribution, you control the product. As a businessman with a choice, I would much rather control the distribution than the manufacturing process.

If I am importing a product and I have distribution for that product—whether I'm selling to jobbers, to stores, or selling direct—I control the product.

How difficult is it for the exporter to replace my distribution? If it is very difficult, I have great control. If it is simple, then I have no control. If I have what is aptly called controlled distribution, then that exporter is vulnerable to me.

When we set up the American distribution system of drop-shipping merchandise in France, we manufactured and shipped directly to the customers. We were, in effect, making the French distributors dependent upon us. When they could buy the merchandise anywhere, imprint it themselves, and so on, they were independent of a manufacturer. But the system was also inefficient. When the distributors joined into our system, in which we manufactured, imprinted, and delivered to the customers, they could devote more time to selling, cut their overhead, expand their marketplace, and make more money. But the one thing they could consider negative was that they were dependent on us. And because it worked so well for them, we became difficult to replace.

If I am exporting, I want as much distribution as I possible can get, so as not to be vulnerable to a single importer. It is exactly the opposite for the importer. The need of the distributor is exclusivity; the need of the manufacturer or exporter is diversification. One of the primary goals of business is to avoid vulnerability as much as possible. As an exporter or manufacturer, the less distribution you have, and more vulnerable you are, even if a single distributor gave you all the business you could handle.

It doesn't happen much anymore, but at one time a giant company like Sears Roebuck could have destroyed a manufacturer. The manufacturer would start selling to Sears. Sears would like the product and take all the manufacturer's output, so the manufacturer would expand and expand—all for one customer. Later, the market would change, someone else would come out with a better product, and suddenly Sears would stop buying from this particular manufacturer. What does the manufacturer do with this factory, its people, the debts it took on to expand?

It is an enormous temptation for a manufacturer. A big company says, "I'll take your entire production. You don't need a sales force, or promotion, or anything. Just make the product and ship it to me, and I'll send you a check." I know a man who has done tremendously well over the past 30 years selling only to Sears. But to me, he is sitting on the brink. I could never make myself susceptible to one outlet. If you have two outlets, you are twice as well off; if you have a thousand outlets, you are a thousand times better off.

It is wise to remember, however, that you can never completely control your distributors. The farther away from you they are, the more difficult it becomes. If you want your distributors to adhere to a particular marketing strategy, you can build it into your sales contract, but you are severely limited in what you can accomplish.

For example, you can specify the market in which you want the product sold. If you are granting an exclusive or a franchise, the distributor can stand to lose it if he usurps your directions. But in the United States—and to some extent almost everywhere in the world—there are restraint-of-trade laws. If you buck those laws you can have a lawsuit on your hands. You can build subtle conditions into your sales contract that enable you to discontinue sales to a particular distributor if he acts to destroy the product image or marketplace, but those conditions are very difficult to enforce.

The best way to handle these problems is to know who your distributors are and trust their integrity. A good agreement assures you as much as can be that the distributor will fulfill the terms. Even so, it still takes great effort, constant supervision, or frequent checks to ensure the job is being done.

Choosing Your Distributor

When I look at a distributor, I don't give a damn if he has 20 warehouses and 3,000 salespeople. I want to know if he can sell my product and pay his bills. Those are the most important things.

There are times when you may not want the biggest and most powerful distributor. Your poor little product might have to scuffle to find a place in his scheme of things. You might be better off finding a hungry guy, someone who needs a new and exciting product and has the temperament to hustle it. Generally, however, when looking for a distributor I assess who has done the biggest job for a comparable item. I don't use my time and money to give people on-the-job training. I would rather go after the guy who has the best track record selling my type of product. If I can't get him, I'll go to the guy who has the second-best track record, and so on in succession.

When you find your distributor, remember that this is not a marriage or some other lifelong commitment. The biggest mistake is to say, "now is forever." You're not stuck with anyone for your entire business life—and shouldn't be, by either inference or contract.

The simplest move is to sell to an importer on a non-exclusive basis. If he buys, fine. If not, you find someone to replace him. Most distributors, however, will ask for exclusivity if they think the product has anything going for it. It gives them time to develop the marketplace and, if there's no competition, they have the ingredients for greater profits. As a manufacturer or exporter, however, I do not want to be vulnerable to one individual, unless I have a three- or five-year contract which guarantees all the merchandise I want to ship into that area.

There are times when exclusivity is a valuable selling tool. The scenario could go something like this: the distributor asks for an exclusive and you say, "How many will you buy?"

"I could probably use a lot," he says.

"I want to know exactly. I'd like to take an order," you say. Never ask for projections or hypothetical numbers. The best and only test is an order. That's a real commitment.

You negotiate the deal. You look in your charts to see what you can produce and what you'd like to get out of the area. Then you word the deal so that, to have the exclusive each year, the distributor has to fulfill the volume commitments. Depending on the product and if it's an expanding market, he could take 100,000 pieces in the first year, 150,000 pieces in the second, 200,000 in the third, and so on. You are satisfied knowing that you've escalated your market. The year the distributor doesn't fulfill the quota, he loses the exclusive and you're free to sell it elsewhere. That's a fair deal.

You'll find that it usually doesn't happen that quickly, however. More often than not, the distributor or importer will buy 10,000 pieces to test the market. You'll give him a 90-day exclusive, followed by an order for 100,000 on an exclusive basis, as outlined above.

But everything doesn't have to be absolute. If the distributor can't handle the volume you want, give him a limited exclusive. You could give him an exclusive in the Paris area, sell exclusively to another distributor in the south of France, one for the central part, and yet another for the north. Now you have four exclusive distributors by territory in one country, and vulnerability is less of a factor because all your eggs aren't in one basket.

The important point is to find a distributor with whom you can work. If you know one by reputation and feel you can trust his ability to fulfill agreements based on his track record, so much the better. If that's not possible, then gut feelings come into play. Sometimes they are as reliable as anything else.

Making Your Distributor Work Hard

You have convinced a distributor to take on your product. He has committed himself by ordering a certain quantity. Your problem is that he also handles a hundred other product lines. How are you going to ensure that your product doesn't languish in his catalog, that his sales force wants to sell it, and that he will order more?

The first way to get a distributor's attention is with profit. Try to make your product more profitable than other items on his normal list. Make him work for that profit by putting the discount on a sliding scale. If he buys $100,000 worth, his discount is 40 percent, but he will get volume rebates when he orders $200,000 worth, or $300,000, or $400,000, and so on. You are not giving him more than anyone else, but you are encouraging him to sell more. If he sells more, he makes an additional profit. The volume rebate goes right to his bottom line; he doesn't have to share it with anyone. It is a simple incentive.

The second way is to make it as easy as possible for a distributor to sell your product. Provide all the auxiliary materials he needs—brochures, point-of-sale items, case histories, good photographs, newspaper veloxes, anything you can think of that will make the presentation to his customers easier. It's one of selling's basic rules: Make it as easy as possible for someone to buy. Set up your ordering system as simply as possible for the distributor. Better yet, make it fit his system, so it's no big deal for him to put in the line.

What about the sales force? You have made your point with the distributor, but he hasn't the ability, desire, or incentive to put it out as strongly to his sales force. First, try to address the sales force directly, as though it were your own sales force. Give them a sales seminar, show them how to sell the product, and, if possible, have detail people actually go into the field with the salespeople and show them how to sell your product.

Second, provide the salespeople with something that will make your product stand out. Maybe it is a special little gift that they use in the pursuit of their daily business: a special folder for their papers, a special portfolio in which to carry their samples, a special, easier order form, or even something as simple as a good writing pen. Put something in those salespeople's hands to constantly remind them of you and your product.

Third, come up with an incentive over and above their regular salaries, commissions, or bonuses—something that says, "Sell this and you get something special." Sometimes it is as simple as money, points toward an incentive vacation, or credits for gifts in a catalog. The incentive should be something over and above what the salespeople normally earn, so it turns them on to sell your particular product.

Once you have your program set, promote the hell out of it. If it is a sales incentive trip that could excite their spouses, send the mailings to their homes. Even address the mailing to the spouse: "Dear Cynthia, Get Bob off his ass and be in Hawaii next month, basking in the sun—all on us." Next time Bob sleeps late, Cynthia may just poke him in the ribs and tell him to get out there and sell, so she can visit Hawaii soon.

These incentive programs should always be done with the advice and consent of the distributor. If you've already persuaded him that he is going to make more profit on your items, and that it is going to be easier to process them than anyone else's lines, the distributor will be only too willing to let you motivate his sales force.

Distribution is the most important segment of your marketing mix. Without it your product goes nowhere. Never forget to tell your distributors you love them. They are important to you, wherever they are, however large they are. Treat them well and, whenever the opportunity becomes available, let them know you care.

Your program also depends in part upon the dynamics of your product. If your distributor sells to retail stores and the consumer isn't buying, all your efforts are for naught. The retailer isn't going to order more if he already has the product on the markdown rack. So the next phase is to motivate retailers and consumers to buy. Remember, however, that there are just so many incentives you can offer; after those, you are going to run out of profit. Still, there are things that can be done.

The first thing—and this is the job of your detail people or the sales force, depending upon your resources—is to get the best piece of real estate in the store. You want your product in the place where there is the most traffic, where the item is most easily seen, or at an impulse spot such as right beside the cash register.

Unfortunately, not only in the United States but also all over the world, there is less and less "selling" done at the retail level. What moves a product is not the clerk, but how the product is positioned and the attractiveness of the point-of-sale display. It is worth investing in both of these elements.

You can also put together promotions to move your product. Gift-with-sale promotions are very popular today, especially with cosmetics. Essentially, they are premiums. If a consumer buys the product, he or she gets something free or for substantially less than the retail price.

There is also general advertising. If you have the margin in your product to do so, it is much nicer for the consumer to walk into a store and ask for your product by name. That is the preselling benefit of general advertising. But in this area particularly, the neophyte (and many experienced businessmen) can land on a merry-go-round, throwing a lot of money around with very little return. I go into more detail on advertising in Chapter 12.

A Complete Package

In today's competitive and jaded marketplace, nothing stands alone—not advertising, nor promotion, nor distribution, nor sales techniques. They are all part of the whole. Marketing strategies have to consider the whole picture; you can't treat only one part. The product, style, distribution, sales, and perceived value all come into play. If the marketing all works, then you have a product that breaks on the scene with a bang, à la the Swatch watch.

Swatch is one of the greatest examples of successful international marketing. The Swiss watch industry, which is the country's basic industry, was being destroyed by competition from the Orient and by the new digital technology. The Swiss had owned the watch market around the world, particularly in better watches. But along came digital technology, and complex movements gave way to quartz. Watches were no longer repaired. With the cost of labor as it was, it was more expensive to repair a watch than to throw it away and get a new one. Suddenly the Swiss watch industry was virtually dead.

Then some people came up with the bright idea of the Swatch. They would use existing technology to put a quartz movement in an analog watch. With a production system totally automated from beginning to end and upbeat modern styling, these new Swiss watches would cost only $30. The Swatch made an enormous international impact, expanded the entire marketplace, and resuscitated the Swiss watch industry. All it took was one simple idea and the marketing expertise to carry it out.

Remember that distribution is not a closed shop. It's difficult to pin down sometimes, because the alternatives today are so numerous. But the old, standard textbook rule of, "Okay, your distribution is: broker, distributor, jobber, retail store, consumer: is not necessarily correct. You can't be narrow-minded or have preset notions. It isn't that simple. Which way should your product go? If you have an atypical product and your investigations find only typical distribution outlets, should you use them? If you go into typical distribution, you might end up with a typical product. In that case, you may want to find another method of distribution.

The alternatives are numerous. Do as many major companies like Mary Kay and Avon have done, and go direct. Sell through multilevel marketing, as Herbalife does. You can sell by catalog, through mail order, and, the latest system, through home shopping on television.

The marketplace has changed drastically in recent years. New techniques, new hardware, and new technology have made merchandising that was formerly impossible now entirely possible and profitable. But you are in a highly complex market, with more outlets, more people who will buy, a larger marketplace than has ever existed, and more competition. You have to stay on top of developments in technology as well as in the marketplace.

This takes me full circle to my primary message in this book. The way to expand your marketplace is to expand your distribution. One way Americans can expand their marketplace is to look overseas for larger markets, new products, different technology, and fresh inspiration. The world has become both a small place and a large market. To remain viable, businessmen can no longer choose *if* they want to export or import. It's a necessity we ignore at our peril.

11

Making the Sale

The importance of sales cannot be overestimated. You can have an idea, and you can even have a product, but nothing happens until someone sells it.

Selling is the basic ingredient of business, whether domestic or international. It involves finding the prospects, getting their attention, presenting your product, and closing the sale.

The basics of selling are the same everywhere. You find a need and fill it. But all the elements just mentioned must be present to bring that about. You have to find the "hot" button of the prospective buyer—usually an unexpressed need. What is there about what you have to sell that will turn a buyer on? What kind of need will your product fill? How do you get the buyer's attention? How do you present your product in the most effective manner? And how do you overcome the natural inertia in all of us, and get that buyer to sign on the dotted line so you can walk away with an order?

The laurels in selling don't go to the loudest talkers or the fastest tap dancers. Good selling takes intelligence, perception, instinct, timing, and a true understanding of the buyer's needs. It's no accident that top salesmen are among the highest income-earners in our society, and that those who have the ability to close sales are the top earners among salesmen. These are skilled and valuable people.

Sales techniques are as unlimited and as varied as human imagination. But they all stem from the same basic principles of selling, and they are all aimed toward the most difficult part of selling—closing the deal. It doesn't matter what the product is; if you don't close the deal, it doesn't get sold. This simple and obvious fact gets overlooked surprisingly often, even though sooner or later it becomes impossible to avoid.

Selling Writing Instruments

One of our companies sells Pierre Cardin writing instruments in an intensely competitive area. There are many fine pens on the market. How do we make our pens stand out? Do we find an exclusive distributor to carry our products, or do we get a distributor who carries many products to feature ours?

The first step is research. Know your competitors. Find out what else is on the market, because that is what you have to sell against. You don't have to use your competitor's name, or even compare your product to his, but you have to understand the market.

Before I make the presentation, my next step is to list all the advantages of my product:

1. It's styled better.
2. It's new.
3. Because it is new, neither he nor his customers have seen anything quite like it.
4. It has a special point-of-sale display to make it prominent.
5. Because Pierre Cardin's name is recognized as a gift item, the pen can sell in parts of the store other than just the stationery department.
6. The designer name has glamour, is attractive to the eventual user.

7. The greatest number of pens are bought, not by users, but as gifts for others. Those who want gifts with the greatest impact will choose this pen over others.

Not a bad string of advantages for the buyer. Now I look at my disadvantages. I won't talk about them, but I must understand them before I attempt to sell the product. In this case, my disadvantages are almost the other side of the coin.

1. Although he is the world's foremost designer, Pierre Cardin is not a recognized pen name. People who go to buy a pen are more likely to have the idea they want a Parker, Mont Blanc, or Cross.
2. The fact that the pen is perceived as a gift rather than a pen could be a limitation.
3. The quality is no better than any other pen—only the styling is different and, in my own opinion, better.
4. We are bucking anywhere from 25 to 100 years of advertising value on the established names.

If any of these disadvantages are brought up during the presentation, I know how to handle them. For example, if the distributor mentions that Pierre Cardin is not an established pen name, I say, "Exactly! More than sixty percent of all pens bought are for gifts. When the recipient gets a box marked Cross or Parker, he knows it's a pen. And he probably knows exactly what it looks like. The excitement has gone. But when he gets a beautiful Pierre Cardin box, he doesn't know what's in it. He still has ahead of him the excitement of discovery."

How do I build my sales presentation? The best presentation is one that can be made *within 60 seconds*. If you can't make a presentation in less than a minute, you are getting too complicated. People don't have the time or attention span to hear long-winded stories. They want the punch line, and they want it fast.

Here's what I'd say: "We've made a dramatic breakthrough in the pen business. We actually got the top designer in the world to design a brand-new pen. We've taken all the techniques of the old-line pen manufacturers to make it technically perfect, but it also has a great look. We've built these attractive point-of-sale displays; we've got a special introductory offer; and, most important, you can make more money with Pierre Cardin pens than with any other."

Boom! End of story. That's all they want to hear. I use essentially the same pitch, whether seeking an exclusive or a general distributor. After that, you can get into the details of the deal.

For example, if I were going to an exclusive pen distributor-importer, who I want to handle the Pierre Cardin pens exclusively, my story would now take a different direction. I would tell him that we had investigated his reputation and his capability, and if he were to take the pens as an exclusive product, we could give him a lot of incentives to make it worthwhile. In selling this pen, he would control an area of business that he might never have controlled before. Why? Because I know there is no way for him to get an exclusive with any of the other brand names. Finally, since we are introducing this new product and need that special push, we will work very closely with him to put the pen into the marketplace.

The distributor is interested only in profit. He wants to know what the newest, best-looking, most prestigious item is. You'll notice we didn't even mention writing quality. All pens write, and the difference in quality is slight. The main hurdle is that although Pierre Cardin is a recognized name, it is not a name associated with pens.

An entirely new level of difficulty ensues when you try to break into the marketplace with an unknown product, such as when we first entered the European markets with our gold Florentine pen. Our main advantage in that case was cosmetic: the look and perceived value of the product. We had a low-priced pen with an excellent finish. It looked expensive, felt expensive, and had the weight of an expensive product. It was different enough from anything else on the market to succeed.

If possible, when entering the market with a new product, stay away from presenting a "me too" item. If you try to sell someone a product that is similar, and almost the same price, as something he already has, you face a tough selling job, regardless of how good you are. The only incentive you can offer is price and—more often than not—you can't offer much there. Try to tailor your line so it doesn't fall into the "me too" bracket. If you don't have the advantages of a brand name, your product should have some benefit that is different.

I always try to avoid selling on the straight basis of price, because I know that eventually I will lose, unless I am willing to put up tons of money to develop a new or patentable technology and the corresponding advertising and promotional funds that will almost certainly be needed. Soon after we opened our European operations, my European agent suggested we buy some new automated equipment. We could get a great deal on it, he said, and it would not only enable us to produce a huge number of pens each hour, but bring the price down to about one cent a pen.

I vetoed the proposal immediately. It would have changed the face of our business and made us a price company. If we had a machine that could produce volume like this, anyone else could get a similar machine. It would be only a matter of time before someone got an even faster machine that could produce the pens even cheaper. At that point we would again have to invest in faster and more efficient automated equipment, and so on, and so on. We would be investing substantial sums of money to keep "me too" items competitive. This wasn't the business I chose. Unless you're comfortable with a low-margin, highly competitive product, you are better off trading something with a unique quality.

Never get caught up in the belief that you're such a great salesman you can sell anything. If you're that great, you'll do much better selling a product that has a market niche or is a one-of-a-kind item, or that has some qualities which set it apart from the rest. Why make it hard on yourself?

Making It Easy—for the Buyer

As I've mentioned earlier, make it as easy as possible for a buyer to say yes. If I find a great distributor of pens in Belgium, for instance, but he is unfamiliar with importing, I have two choices. Either I find an importer to import the pens and then sell them to him, or I find a way to import them myself into that country and then sell them to him. I do not persuade him to become an importer.

People are very uncomfortable with the unknown. I don't want to teach a buyer a new technology of business. I'd have to sell him first on the product, then on becoming an importer. I'd rather make it easy for him to say yes. If I have a good product, I first have to present it to him in as clear and uncomplicated a manner as possible. Once he is sold on that, my second job is to structure the deal so that it's easy for him.

If the buyer is a super-mover of merchandise, but he is not too well capitalized, the extension of credit terms can be part of the sale. For example, "Well, Mr. Gaston," I would say, "I think that, given a chance, you could sell a lot of my product, which would be good for both of us. In order to help you penetrate the marketplace, I'll give you ninety-day terms."

This is a big incentive. He doesn't have to finance the deal; instead he can turn over his receipts and pay me out of what he gets paid. It's easy for him.

On the other hand, if your prospect is well heeled and has no problem with cash, offer him a discount for prompt payment. You could even offer a larger discount for advance payment.

Selling isn't pulling a swift con job. It's knowing what the customer needs, knowing what you have that could fill those needs, and making it as easy as possible for him to buy.

The "Hot" Button

When I first started Jack Nadel, Inc., I trained all new salesmen myself by going out with them and making calls, usually cold calls. On one particular day, I went with a new salesman who had experience with other lines but not with the specialty advertising business.

We called on Republic Insurance, a company in Los Angeles, and met with two old partners who sat at desks facing each other. I tried to sell them a leather-covered desk calendar, and I thought I had them. They really liked the product. I told them about the advantages—how the customers would really like it, and how the calendar would stay on their desks 365 days of the year, constantly reminding them of Republic Insurance. Every time I outlined a benefit, each partner would look up and nod, saying, "Gee, that really is good."

But I couldn't close them. I just couldn't do it. "May I take your order? It's a dated item; may I reserve some for you?"

"No. No."

I tried every close I could think of, but none worked. It was exasperating, because I knew they wanted it. I just couldn't find their "hot" button—the idea or words that would turn them on to it.

Suddenly the trainee salesman, who hadn't opened his mouth during the entire conversation, spoke. "If you sign the order now, we'll put the imprint of your company name on it at no charge," he said.

One partner looked at the other. He nodded. "Okay," the first one said. "That's a good deal."

Well, in our business the imprinting comes along with the deal. It's part of the overall price. But this salesman found a button that I didn't know existed. In my smooth and experienced presentation, I simply had neglected to mention the obvious (I thought) fact that the imprint was a part of the deal.

It was a valuable lesson. The "hot" button is always there. It doesn't always make sense to you, but that's immaterial. It makes sense to the person who is buying, and that's what is important. All you have to do is find it.

How do you do that? The best way is the simplest. If you don't already know the "hot" button, ask. There are a number of questions you can interject into the conversation:

"If you could write the deal with everything that you want in it, what would you like to have?"

"If I were your fairy godfather and I could give you anything, what would you want?"

"What is your biggest problem?"

"What can I do to make it easier for you to use this product?"

"How can I make this more profitable for you?"

It is amazing how people respond when you ask these simple questions. The key is in not taking an adversarial position, but in getting on the same side of the desk as the buyer. Look at a problem together and solve it together.

If you are active in the market, you don't have to ask what the problems are; you already know them. In any particular business, the problems are generally universal. As a professional in that same business, you try to solve those problems in your merchandising. If I had taped conversations I had 20 years ago in the United States and compared them with ones last month in Europe, you'd see that the problems are still the same.

In the advertising specialty business, everyone is looking for new products. European and Oriental distributors particularly travel all over the world to find new products. If you can bring a new product of merit to them, you will have hit their "hot" button.

The second common "hot" button has nothing to do with selling a product, but rather is how the buyer can keep his costs down so he can make a better profit. Everything has to be geared to profit. That's why people are in business.

In making a presentation I address myself only to two things: making the sale and increasing the profit potential for my customer.

How can he make a higher percentage of profit? How can he sell much more of my product? How can he better penetrate the market? How can he get a higher percentage of the marketplace? These are all buzzwords that turn people on. Essentially, what you are always saying is, "I can provide something for you through my product or service that is going to increase your profit without making you uncomfortable."

Comfort is a very important concept in business. If I offer you a million dollars to jump off the top floor of the Empire State Building, it will make you very uncomfortable. But you could make a million dollars. There are much more comfortable ways to make a million dollars, and it's those you look for.

You can't break a normal person's routine. Understand that the bulk of the marketplace is not made up of forward thinkers and pioneers, and you can't turn them into that. If a man is in the business of selling pens to retail stationery stores, and I can offer him a better pen at a better price, it will be in his comfort zone and he will consider it. But if I come to him with a new product that is a pen on one side and a bottle opener on the other, I immediately make him uncomfortable because he's not in the bottle-opener business.

Businessmen want products that will make them the greatest profit with the least inconvenience and discomfort. It comes back to the basic principle of making it easy for him to buy. Address yourself to his problems and solve them; don't create new problems for him to solve. Find the "hot" button and use it constructively. You'll have a new customer.

Urgency

A cardinal rule of international sales is that if an offer (which may contain catalogs, specifications, or materials) is going to a qualified prospect, it is always sent by overnight delivery. After that comes a telex message. And, if I think it makes sense, I pick up the phone and call.

I want to take my business out of the realm of the ordinary and endow it with a sense of urgency. Everyone in business receives reams of mail each day. I want my communications to stand out, and the additional cost of express mail versus ordinary air mail is very small compared to the attention it will get.

As strange as it may seem in our modern age, people around the world are still impressed when they receive a telephone call from the United States. At times, I even set it up with a telex: "Thanks for your reply to my letter of ——. There are still a few things that need to be explained. I will telephone you at 9 A.M., your time, on Tuesday morning, ——." The buyer responds by telex, and we have the discussion at the pre-set date. He is ready and waiting.

To someone who has been in business for 40 years, it's remarkable that today you can send your samples by courier service and have them delivered pretty much anywhere in the world within 48 hours. It used to cost hundreds of dollars to do that; now it's around $40. If you're willing to give it three or four days, the cost is only about $15. If you are involved in international business, some marvelous tools are available: direct-dial telephone, telex, FAX, courier services. Use them all.

Use discretion, of course. These services all cost money. If you're doing a general solicitation to distributors around the world, use regular air mail. It's merely an introduction to prospects who may not be exactly hot. But if you have something special to sell and you need fast answers, pick your ten best prospects and send your samples with the offering by the fastest way possible.

Your sense of urgency says "Tomorrow isn't good enough. You must have the product in your hands as soon as possible, because the market is perfect right now and the competition is waiting." Not only do I make the solicitation urgent, but I create an environment that urges the buyer to order immediately and press for immediate delivery.

You want your prospect's 100 percent attention. Along the same line, when you make an appointment with a buyer in a foreign country, call ahead and make sure he has set time aside for you. Have the time blocked out, so that you have his undivided attention, particularly if you have to travel thousands of miles to see him.

The deal is *important,* and the prospect has to know it! Use all the tools at your disposal to impress this fact upon your clients and prospects.

Make Every Call Pay

At the end of the day, I would ask one of my least effective salesmen how he has done.

"I really worked hard today," he might say. "First, I made a call in Santa Monica, then I had to climb in my car and see a prospect in Pasadena. After that I went across town to see someone in Torrance."

"Well," I say, "you spent two hours on sales calls and six hours traveling."

Planning is a vital part of selling, if you're going to use your time most effectively. It's not always possible, but, in this instance, my salesman should have planned his calls so that he covered the west side of Los Angeles at one time, and the east side of the city at another.

When doing business on an international scope, this becomes even more important. If you are going to London, Paris, and Frankfurt, how are you going to make the trip pay? There's a ratio between your time and expenses and your number of sales calls, and it can't grow lopsided. This takes planning.

When I was younger I used to think I was a superman. I would fly to London on the evening plane, get in the next morning with little or no sleep, quickly shave and shower in my hotel room, and then make a call. I thought I was a real bull. I thought I was bright and sparkling. Now I think I looked terrible. And I was doing a real disservice to the product line I had to sell. Now I know I am much more effective if, after I arrive, I spend the day doing nothing but getting rid of jet lag, instead of yawning in the buyer's face.

Presentation

Another aspect of sales that involves planning is the presentation. I hate to admit to the times I've traveled 3,000 or 6,000 miles to open my case in front of a buyer, only to find that my sample doesn't work. Just about everyone has been on one side or the other of that situation, and it's the most embarrassing thing in the world—for both seller and buyer.

It's a simple matter that a surprising number of people overlook. Prepare your samples so that they are absolutely perfect—before you leave. Too many salesmen go to the sample department, ask them to put together a kit, and never look at it. Hell, they know what's in the kit; perhaps they even created it. So they don't examine the contents, and they end up looking like idiots before the client. The presentation should start with an examination of the product in the privacy of your office. Make sure it is shiny, squeaky clean, and works perfectly.

The major part of selling is in the preparation. It's like an hour-long rehearsal for a one-minute speech. But if you've done your planning well, the 60-second presentation is dynamite.

The presentation is much like writing a letter. The opening has to grab the prospect. "Mr. Buyer, I've got a terrific idea that's going to increase your business." Or, "Mr. Buyer, I've got a great product that will increase your profits." Or, "Mr. Buyer, I've got a new item that will be grabbed up in the marketplace very quickly."

The lead statement has to get his attention, and it always has to show a direct benefit to the customer. When you have his interest, you can show the product.

The product itself should always be in its best possible dress. Even a relatively inexpensive product should be set against a beautiful background. I can simply hold up a pen; or I can put it against a piece of black or red suede. Throw the shiniest diamond on a table, and it will look like nothing;

but put an inexpensive fake diamond against a decent background, and it will look marvelous.

Unless you're dealing with some highly technical product, the verbal presentation should be done in less than a minute. Salesmen come into my office and bore the hell out of me. They tell me about their tremendous production facilities, or they open with a golf story, or they waste time telling me about the technical excellence of their product. They wind up doing themselves a horrible disservice.

All I want to know is: (1) Can I buy it and sell it? (2) Can I make a good profit on it? and (3) Is it a good product I'll be proud to sell? I don't care how or where it's made— or what the salesman's golf score is. All I'm interested in is what it looks like, how it works, and whether or not it's a good buy.

Within six months after I started selling as a young man, I called on a guy who had a placard on his desk, which I never forgot. I didn't write it down, but it stuck in my mind. It said: "Samson killed 2,000 Philistines with the jawbone of an ass, but that's nothing remarkable. Every day, thousands of sales are killed with the same instrument." Keep your presentation short.

Solving His Problem

For some time, Parker dominated the pen market. In fact, when I went to Asia in the fifties and sixties, I discovered that people were selling Parker pen caps—without the pens— and doing a great business. Chinese businessmen would wear the caps in their shirt pockets to show the distinctive Parker arrow. God knows what would happen if you asked to borrow the pen. There was nothing there, just the prestigious cap.

It was 1976, and we had a problem with an important distributor in Brussels. This was the leading specialty distributor in Belgium, a company run by two brothers, Jacques and Jean. The distributor was doing little with our Pierre Cardin line of pens, so I stopped in to see them. They very proudly took me through their showroom, which exhibited almost every specialty product available in Europe. The most prominent display was for the Parker Pen Company.

It gave me a clue. Amidst this mass of merchandise, it was our major competitor that had the featured position. "Jacques," I said, "I see you've got a beautiful Parker display there. That's a really terrific line of pens, isn't it?"

"They are the best pen, but I've had difficulty with them," he said.

"Oh? What's your problem?"

"The customer wants the pen, but, as you know, there is very little profit," he said disgruntedly.

"I see the problem," I said. "Also, doesn't Parker sell direct?"

"Oh, yes," he said. "They sell direct, too."

"The company is basically in competition with you, isn't it?" I said.

"Yes, basically."

And that was his problem. I had the solution. "It's going to take a lot more effort," I said, "but with our Pierre Cardin pens, you can make three times the profit that you can with Parker, and if you become the key person here selling Pierre Cardin, we will always give you a special position in our company."

He asked me to explain. "Well, at the beginning, to introduce the pen, you get a full discount on all quantities. And once you've sold the pen, you can be sure that we will never compete with you directly, because that's our policy."

"If I.B.M. Belgium calls you direct, you mean you wouldn't sell to them?"

"Absolutely not. We would refer the inquiry to you," I said, adding, "The most important thing, Jacques, is that we can build a permanent business that will give you more profit on a protected basis. You will never have a problem with us because we are specialty people who went into the pen business, whereas Parker is a pen company that went into the specialty business. I know its product is terrific, but the name of your game is profit, isn't it?"

"But yes," he said.

They liked the idea, but I decided to make it even easier for them to say yes. "Give me the names of your best customers and their imprint. At my own expense, I will put their imprint on the Pierre Cardin pen, and you can present it to them. If they don't buy it, then it will just be my risk, not yours. But instead of making 17 percent you will make 40 percent on the orders."

"How can we lose?" Jacques said.

"You can't," I said. "Sign here."

Jacques and Jean are two of my close friends. We visit each other regularly, and Jean's son worked for one year in our Providence factory so that he could understand the manufacturing process. Plus, they remain our best customer in Belgium. They have done very well with the Pierre Cardin line.

I knew what the problem was before I walked in to see them. Parker was on the decline. It had antagonized the specialty trade in Europe by selling directly to the distributors' customers. And it had built a minimum profit for the distributors into their line, because of the money it had to spend on consumer advertising. All I had to do was solve the problem and get the order.

Getting to the Top

Early in my career, I made a presentation to the assistant sales promotion manager at Hughes Aircraft. Hughes was a giant company, and the possibilities were tantalizing. The man loved my product line and thought it would be a terrific idea for the company. He was very enthusiastic.

"However, we can't present it to *management* like this," he said. It sounded as if he were talking about God. He wanted me to draw up a complete proposal, together with samples of each of the products. "I'll turn them over to Engineering and have them mount each sample on a Lucite board. Under the board we'll title exactly what the product and price are. It'll look gorgeous."

The presentation took six more calls on my part. I can't even count the hours the engineers spent constructing the presentation. But finally it was ready and my friend said, "Now I will take it to *management.*"

The executive who really made the decisions was a retired Air Force general. I asked the assistant sales promotion manager if I could go with him.

"Oh, no," he objected. Apparently *management* rarely saw mere mortals.

He gained admittance into the inner sanctum while I stationed myself outside the door. I'm a believer in fast presentations, but this was ridiculous. It took all of 20 seconds! He went in with the display representing hundreds of manhours and a pint of my blood, and he said, "General, I have a terrific giveaway program."

The general looked up from his desk and said, "Hell, no!" And that was the end of that.

I made two major mistakes. The first was not trying hard enough to see the real decision maker, and the second was allowing myself to be taken in by the enthusiasm of someone who *could not* make the decision. Always find the right guy. Who is the right guy? He is the person who has the authority to single-handedly give you the order.

Always try to call on the person who makes the decision. He doesn't have to justify that decision to anyone or sell it to anyone else. If you are selling something that hasn't been handled by the company before and there is no easy means of comparison, the last person to see is the purchasing agent. Go to the man who can make the decision, and tell him your story. Start with the owner or president and work your way down the ladder. Obviously, the president isn't going to buy paper clips and stationery supplies, so you have to find the person authorized to make that decision.

If at all possible, stay away from committees. If two people make the decisions, you have four times the problems. If four people make the decisions, your problem is 16 times more complex. It expands geometrically, not arithmetically. The more people it takes to reach a unanimous decision, the worse off you are.

If you are persistent enough, you usually can reach anyone. Start with a letter to introduce yourself, requesting an interview and stating how you can make or save money for the firm. If necessary, graduate to a mailgram or telegram. If you still have had no response, call him.

If you start at the bottom, you will rarely, if ever, get to the top. If you start at the top, you may get sent down, but at least it will come with the president's approval—and that has some weight. If you have a new deal, concept, or product to sell, talk to the guy who can buy.

Closing the Sale

People get a curious paralysis, as yet undiagnosed by the medical profession, between the time you put a pen in their hand and they lower it to sign on the dotted line. "Wait a minute," they say. "Let's talk about this some more." Through the years you learn to cure this paralysis, and you become a good salesman.

How do you get an order? How do you get people to make a decision? Deciding is the toughest thing for most people. You can capture their attention and get them excited, but then one of a thousand reasons comes along for them not to decide. "Try me again in another month," or, "Let me sleep on it." Every salesman has heard hundreds more. They are all reasons to postpone a decision.

When the person who is supposed to be the decision-maker says, "Let me sleep on it and give it some thought," I invariably say, "Okay, you've slept on it. What do you know now that you didn't know yesterday?" He knows no more, of course. It is simply a fear of making a decision, a fear of making a mistake. It's the salesperson who can help him overcome this fear and get the decision made.

How? Well, this isn't a primer on sales techniques, so I will only mention a few. Every salesman has his favorites—the ones that work for him—and they are all designed to get the prospect over that hump of indecision. Here are some closing lines I've used:

"If you sign the order, I'll have it in your warehouse next week. Time is of the essence."

"The product is so good it'll soon be in the hands of your competition. Be the first."

"The market is right. Get it out and working for you right now."

And so on. One of the most valuable techniques is based on the mysterious fact that, for some reason, people refuse to tell you the real reason they don't want to buy what you have to sell. A buyer might say, "I can't buy now because I'm overstocked," and I would never accept it. I reply, "I understand your objections, but, besides that, why don't you want to buy now?" *Besides that.* More often than not, he will tell me the real reason.

Another technique is to use the word *reserve*. If the person is teetering on the edge, I'll say, "Well, I'll tell you what. Let me reserve 1,000 pieces for you." And I'll write up the order and he will sign it. The word *reserve* is somehow less threatening than, "Give me an order." Sometimes it pays to find a synonym. You're not hoodwinking the customer; it simply is that he doesn't like to give an "order."

Once a customer has given an order, set the stage for the next order, because you will never be in a better situation than after you've gotten a signed order. At that point you both feel good, and the customer is receptive. That's when I say, "This is going to be great, but now let's talk about the future."

When closing decisions involve committees, it is even more difficult. I remember once calling on one of the largest savings and loans associations in the United States—American Savings and Loan—run by the legendary financial figure Mark Taper. He didn't have time to see me in his office, so he invited me to his home in Beverly Hills.

He had a meeting in his study with his staff while I waited. I could hear every word. Within ten minutes, they had disposed of $50 million worth of loans! And then I came in with my specialties. It took these financial wizards two hours to decide whether to buy a 20¢ gift. Although Taper was the decision-maker, he elicited opinions from each of his officers. And, of course, each had a different opinion. It was a horror.

At the very outset of my career, I came up with a gimmick to handle a closing when it dragged on too long. I called it a "decisionometer." When the meeting reached the stage where I despaired of ever getting a decision, I'd say, "Mr. Jones, I've got a way of taking the decision out of your hands. I've created a new scientific instrument called a decisionometer."

"What's that?" he'd say.

And with that I would take out a coin I had specially made and toss it in the air.

"It's a coin."

"Wait a minute, you'll see," I'd say, catching the coin and covering it. "Are you ready?"

I would uncover the coin. Written on it were the words *Do It!* Mr. Jones would laugh. "Come on, it says *Do It!* on the other side, too."

I'd hand the coin to him and say, "Look on the other side." He'd take the coin and turn it over to see the words, *To Hell with It!* It always got a good laugh, but there was more to it than that. It said, either do it or forget it; I don't want to come back. Salesmen make one mistake over and over. They are afraid to bring the issue to a head—afraid to get a "no" that will kill the deal then and there. They let it strangle itself to death over the next few months, instead. I would rather get a definitive "no," than a stalling "maybe."

There is a certain point when I feel I've told my story and given the buyer every opportunity to make the decision. Then it's either a yes or a no. If he says "no," he's doing me a favor because I won't waste any more time on him. But if

I make four more calls before he tells me "no" three months later, I really feel miserable about the time I've wasted. I'd rather draw the issue to a close. My decisionometer was my way to bring about a decision.

Sales techniques comprise using everything you have. You use your product, the pricing, the customer's needs, the presentation—every weapon at your diposal. The basics of selling are the same, no matter what the product. You can get as fancy or as complex as you want, but it is often unnecessary. If you ignore the basics, the sale just won't work. But if you build everything on the two principles of filling a need and of making it easy for the customer to say "yes," you'll make your sale.

12

Effective Advertising

The old saying, "Create a better mousetrap and the world will beat a path to your door," is just so much wishful thinking. A lot of people are out there creating better mousetraps. If you want to stand apart from the crowd, you have to let people know that you have a better mousetrap. Advertising is the tool you use to do this.

The purpose of advertising is to reach the people who can buy your goods and services, to let them know how good your product will be for them, and to motivate them to buy it. If you don't advertise in some manner, your product is likely to languish in anonymity.

With the dominance of the mass media these days, people tend to think of advertising in terms of television, newspapers, and magazines, even though these are only a part of the total. Furthermore, if you are entering the market with a product that isn't for general use, or for which you don't have a multimillion dollar budget, this type of mass advertising is either impossible to consider or not necessarily the best way to go.

Much has been written on advertising and the mass media, but it doesn't really apply to millions of small businesses, particularly those who have specialized or limited markets. If you are in the automobile, toothpaste, or laundry detergent business, then everyone in this audience of 240 million Americans is a prospect. In that case, you're willing to pay $400,000 for a television spot during the Superbowl to create an impression on 140 million people. But if you have a limited market and a limited budget, the mass media is not a viable alternative.

Advertising can be a tremendous drain on a business's resources, particularly if it is ineffective. Apart from the cost, the main problem with most mass media advertising is that results are difficult to measure. If you pay $200,000 or $300,000 for a spot on a highly rated television show, you've got to wonder how many people went to the bathroom or the kitchen while your commercial was playing—or, God forbid!, how many used the remote control to turn down the volume or switch the channel. If you invest in a full-page newspaper ad, you've got to wonder how many people actually read it. Yes, you got exposure, but just how much? And will it actually bring people to your door? This is the wondering that brings on ulcers.

Even giant corporations with millions to spend are taking a harder look at their advertising expenditures today. This is reflected in the decline of network television advertising revenues as well as the drop in revenues of the big advertising agencies themselves. It is also reflected in the *increased* revenues of special-interest media such as magazines that cater to segmented markets and radio stations with definable audiences. Mass media takes you to a broad market, many of whose people cannot even use what you have to sell. Smart companies are less interested in nebulous campaigns, and see the wisdom of a more direct attack. People want measurable results.

When I started Measured Marketing Services, the chairman of Republic Corporation told me to come up with a name for this new subsidiary. I went through dozens of lists until finally I asked myself what we actually did. We were a group of companies in the direct-mail, advertising specialty, and premium businesses, and we all had one thing in common— you could actually measure the results of the advertising.

I was elated to come up with Measured Marketing Services as a name. It rolled off my tongue. It stated something that ninety percent of most advertising agencies never do: put themselves on the line to be measured continually as to the results of their advertising. I reported to the chairman the next day with a big smile on my face and presented my sole choice of name.

"It will never fly," he said. I was persistent, however, and the name stuck. We created the concept of putting out a series of advertising promotions of which clients could actually measure the results.

What kinds of advertising is really available for the small businessman today? It's a difficult question to answer. Advertising can be a very potent weapon, but it can also be a dramatic waste of money. How much money do you have to spend? What do you have to sell? What is your marketplace? How do you reach it most economically? What is the best media? And, most important, how do you motivate your public to buy?

Good advertising has to precipitate action. It is mass selling. A creative advertising campaign gets someone to do something. It motivates customers to walk through your door to buy your product or call for your services. It is direct and effective.

Specialty Advertising

Specialty advertising is a type of advertising about which very little is known. It has proved very effective, and has given me a living for many years. Specialty advertising involves a product of some intrinsic value that is used as a giveaway and, it is hoped, retained by the person you are trying to reach.

Something as simple as a calendar or a ballpoint pen imprinted with your name can be given to your prospects. The calendars hang on their walls or sit on their desks for 365 days. If you give a good pen that can be used, your prospects will see your name every time they write with it.

When we started Jack Nadel, Inc., about 50 percent of the business was Christmas gifts. It was, and still is, a damn good habit for business to show their appreciation and extend their good wishes to their customers and clients. Whether it's something as inexpensive as a card or as expensive as a nice gift without an advertising message, it's a wise thing to do.

Specialty advertising is based on the idea that all business is personal. If you have a limited audience and a lot of competition, it helps to be on a personal basis so that—all things being equal—when it comes to the distribution of business, you'll get it.

The major benefit of specialty advertising is that a business goes to an exact marketplace of people who are steady or potential customers. Everything that's put out is directed toward a customer or a prospect, and there is no wasted circulation. It is one of the more expensive forms of advertising, but it is very effective.

The modern extension of this is the premium program, which is also a very measurable, sharp way to advertise. Cosmetic companies use premiums successfully in department stores today. "Buy this collection of cosmetics and get a free bag," or, "Buy twenty dollars worth of cosmetics, and get this skin care collection for only five dollars." You know exactly how much has been bought and how many people were motivated to buy that particular cosmetic.

The frequent-flyer programs run by airlines these days are also premium programs. It is a huge business. "Fly fifty thousand miles on our airline and get a free flight." The airlines know exactly how many people make use of the programs and how many awards they have given. The premium has cost them very little in this case, because all they are doing is giving away empty seats in most cases.

People probably don't realize how many premium programs are being sold these days. They are very effective because they say, "Do this and you get this." The results can be measured. If the program fails, you know it and don't use that program again. There's no guesswork involved.

People love to receive gifts, and they love to get what they perceive as a bargain. Whether the item is an outright gift, as in specialty advertising, or a direct incentive to buy, as in premiums, they will respond positively.

Direct Mail

In 1985, for the first time ever, more money was spent for direct-mail advertising than for television—$21 billion to $20 billion. It's an indication that businesses want to measure what their advertising dollars are bringing in; it's part of a trend away from advertising results that are difficult to measure.

Direct mail is entirely measurable. For the mass of businesses it is the most cost-effective method of advertising. You reach everyone you want to reach, particularly if you have a limited and known marketplace for your products or services.

If I were selling the Rolls-Royce, for instance, I wouldn't bother advertising on television (and they don't), because the vast majority of the viewing audience can't afford the product. Instead, I would find a mailing list of people who are in a qualifying income bracket or, perhaps, who own a Mercedes-Benz and may wish to step up to Rolls-Royce ownership.

Direct mail can be as simple as sending a letter to a couple dozen prospects or as involved as renting mailing lists with millions of names and preparing sophisticated mailing pieces. Either way, it is a message targeted directly to your prospects.

One of the main advantages of direct mail is that the campaign can be tested in small quantities and consequently refined, so that the response can be predicted to an amazing degree. And because the response is exactly measurable, costs per sale can be computed accurately, and therefore a business knows exactly what it is getting for its advertising dollar.

An entirely new term has arisen since the advent of direct mail advertising: junk mail. But anything that people could use can't be called junk. Most people can't use 90 percent of the products advertised on television, yet is that called junk television? Its likely that half the ads in a newspaper won't apply to you, but is that called junk newspaper? Be that as it may, people do get a lot of direct mail. Because of that, one of the initial problems is getting the recipient to open the mail and read the letter containing your offer. The real difficulty is finding an agency that knows how to put your message in the mail in a manner that gets the recipient to act. This takes skill and know-how. But direct-mail advertising is extraordinarily effective if properly done, particularly for a business with a limited budget and a known potential marketplace.

Whether you are new in business or experienced, you can't afford to spend a lot of money reaching people who can't buy what you have to offer. Direct mail is not inexpensive these days, but ultimately it is a cost-effective way of reaching your particular customers.

Direct Response

Direct response can be direct mail, premiums, or any other kind of advertising that calls for an answer. The recipient is asked to act.

A perfect example is a campaign we ran recently for Kelly Services. The purpose of their promotion was twofold: to bring in more temporary personnel, and to let businesses know they are a marvelous source of experienced help. We created a series of mailings to go to two selected groups: existing customers and prospects. Part of the mailing was a contest. If the customer or business sent back the right answer, they got certain premiums or gifts. But they were also getting the message that Kelly is an answer to their problems. The entire promotion was put together to generate a response. Through the direct response, Kelly can trace the business generated by the mailings.

Another program we did identified segments of the market for Apple Computer by sending out pre-approved credit cards that could be applied to the purchase of Apple products. It was a tremendously successful promotion. The program would have been judged a success if Apple had traced between 10,000 and 15,000 computers sold through the card; in this instance, more than 100,000 computers were sold.

Direct response begins with a concept. For Apple, the problem was motivating people to walk into their dealers' stores and buy a computer. The solution was to extend credit to potential buyers. We preselected a public with a good credit rating, and sent them actual credit cards that could be taken into a dealership and used.

Now that is direct response. It is getting someone to do something. It is transactional advertising. And it is an excellent means of advertising because it is measurable.

If one of the major requirements of selling is making the sale as easy as possible, it's the same with advertising. Direct-response advertising gets results, and is a viable alternative for many businesses today.

Brochures

Your brochure is a very important promotional tool. It is also one of the most difficult things to do correctly. Many times brochures are written to satisfy the egos of the writer or the company president, and it does not accomplish its true purpose—selling your product or service.

Self-serving, flowery language falls on deaf ears. People have grown tired of self-hype. Many brochures say too much and oversell the product. If you are selling technical or practical products, the brochure should contain real information. If you are selling glamorous products, there should be more photographs than information. In either case, the brochure follows the same rules as for any good advertising. It has to be catchy, it has to grab attention, and it has to sell the product.

Ninety percent of the self-made brochures I've seen are junk. You must go to an agency or individual who specializes in preparing brochures, and you must judge him by judging what he has done before. It's easy. Examine his previous brochures and see if they have the class and quality you want.

And, as with any advertising, target the brochure to your marketplace. Identify your prospects and slant the brochure toward them. An effective brochure is much more profitable than expanding your ego. You can't go wrong if you remember that the brochure is merely another sales approach to grab attention, sell the product, and ask for the order.

Promotions and Public Relations

Many years ago, I came up with an idea that turned out to be one of the smartest things I had ever done. It was 1959, and major-league baseball came to Los Angeles for the first time. There was a great deal of interest. We always had a couple of professional athletes working for us, and through them we were able to meet the proper people. At the end of each game there was a radio interview, usually with the star of that particular game. And after that interview, a gift was always given to that player for appearing.

I made a deal, first with the Angels, then with the U.C.L.A. Bruins, and later with the Los Angeles basketball team, the Lakers. At the end of the interview the gift was given, along with the comment, "courtesy of Jack Nadel, Inc., the finest company in California for executive gifts."

It was a very short tag line, but the program ran for about four years. The repetition made our name almost generic in California with specialty advertising and executive gifts. And all it cost was the gift itself. With 160 games a year, you couldn't buy effective promotion like that.

Incidentally, we negotiated with the Dodgers, but another company got the program. Yet to this day people still say, "Hey, I remember; you used to sponsor the Dodger games." Because of the constant exposure, people remembered our name.

Closely aligned with promotional programs such as this is the area of public relations. P.R. professionals can place worthy stories about you or your product in newspapers and magazines. The benefit is not only the exposure, but the credibility that goes along with them. Anyone with money can buy advertisements, but when a disinterested observer writes a story about you or your product, it imbues a credibility that people pay attention to.

Like advertising, promotions and public relations efforts require a little ingenuity on your part or the assistance of ingenious professionals in the field. In either case, the payoff in exposure is well worth the expense.

Image

Your brochure, your letterhead, the way your switchboard operator greets callers, the condition of your office, the way you speak to people, how accessible you are, and a dozen other factors all form your image.

Image is what you are. Stores like F.W. Woolworth or Fedco can't put out the same type of brochures, advertising matter, or letterheads as can Tiffany & Co. The former two are appealing to the mass market, while the latter is trying for a very select and wealthy group of people who have seen just about everything there is to see. Your image has to harmonize with what you are selling, with what you are, and with whom you are selling to. Image is something you have, and projecting that image is the job of your advertising, promotion, and public relations.

As I said earlier, there are quality manufacturers and cheap manufacturers; you can't convert one to the other. If a company has a shoddy personality and an immature image, it's almost impossible to change it to a slick, sophisticated image. It's like trying to make someone taller; you can't do it. Maybe you can give him a pair of elevator shoes and make him appear taller, but you can't *make* him taller. As soon as he takes the shoes off, he's his old self again.

Bluffs don't carry for long, either. The image is what you are. It's the job of your advertising and public relations programs to make that image appear positive, so use what you have to its best advantage. If, for instance, you have the common touch, use that as your hook and make it carry your program.

People often make the mistake of trying for a place in the market where they don't belong. The Price Club is a huge discount house with the common touch: They have no frills. They have warehouses full of merchandise at the lowest possible prices. You get a shopping cart, and you haul the stuff out at the best price. They are selling price—nothing else. But if you look at Neiman-Marcus, Tiffany & Co., or Steuben Glass, you'll see they aren't selling price, but elegance. It would be ludicrous to promote Tiffany as having the common touch.

Use everything you have, but don't try to be something you aren't. That's integrity—and people respect it.

Follow-Through

In 1957, we went to a trade fair in Tokyo, where they had executed a great deal of what the textbooks said they should do. There were beautiful booths, expert displays, and glossy promotional materials. But the brochures were all in Japanese. And nobody there spoke English.

The Tokyo fair had been advertised around the world and had drawn a lot of people. But when it finally came down to basics, the organizers hadn't executed their plan. We traveled thousands of miles, spent significant amounts of time and money, only to be frustrated by a lack of communication.

Of course, the Japanese have come a long way since then. Today they are expert at putting on great shows, with facilities that include materials and translators in all major languages. But at that time they had provided a near-ultimate example of a tremendous amount of money spent with very little results—all because they didn't think the situation through to realize that Americans and Englishmen would probably not speak Japanese.

Advertising makes the statement, marketing finds the best way to put it before the public, and sales closes the deal.

Those are the basics. But you have to be prepared to execute at every stage or it all comes to nought. For instance, you can spend a ton of money on advertising, marketing, sales presentations, and sales efforts, but if the product doesn't come up to standard, your money is wasted. You have to fulfill all the promises that were made in the advertising.

We once came out with a product called Crazy Pens. These were a group of novelty ballpoint pens that didn't look like pens until you pulled them apart. There was a nail pen, a ratchet pen, a wrench pen, a heart pen, and many other shapes. Our business was selling advertising, so the name of the advertiser was imprinted on the barrel. There were also some very corny slogans to tie in with the shape like "The best tool for the job," and "Let's get to the heart of the matter," and so on. We had the pens and the equipment to imprint.

It all came out beautifully. The imprint was sharp and attractive, and the pens looked great. The only problem was that the supplier didn't provide us with the right ink, and the imprint came off after a few days. The message was destroyed. No big deal, except the message was the whole reason for the novelty pen and the whole reason for the sale. It all came to nothing.

It happens too often in business. Some little thing you never anticipated louses you up. Before you start a marketing and advertising program, make sure you follow through. Check and double-check everything, from the presentation to the delivery to the quality of the merchandise. After all, you can make the greatest pitch in the world, but you'll never sell a bum product twice.

Experts

If you're like me, you don't believe in on-the-job training at your expense. You want to hire experts to do an expert job. But even while you do this, you have to remember that the so-called experts can be wrong. Award-winning agencies that have produced successful promotions can also turn out big losers. And sometimes you can get caught in such nonsense.

We are supposed to be experts, but we made a mistake as recently as 1982. We introduced the Pierre Cardin writing instruments to the U.S. market, and we decided to advertise the brand. We had a limited budget, so we put out a very nice-looking brochure and also printed statement stuffers for department stores. We hired a highly recommended advertising agency to do the campaign.

One of the partners in the agency was the production manager—a very exacting man. He wanted it to look good, and so did we, but in the process of choosing the models and the paper and the photographs, we spent an unconscionable amount of money. It was out of proportion with any results we could expect to get.

We never got the retail exposure we wanted for the Pierre Cardin pens. We didn't have the budget, and there wasn't enough market to warrant the money we did spend. The product couldn't be sold in enough quantity to merit that kind of exposure. It cost us a great deal of money, and we never got off the ground.

When the agency proposes a program, keep in mind that they have a vested interest. Most regular advertising agencies are interested in clients with large budgets, who are going to buy vast amounts of time and space. The agency gets a commission on it all.

You can buy whatever services you need, but they have to be tailor-made to your product or service. Your campaign has to be like a custom suit—it has to fit. If you know who you are, who your market is, and what you have to say to them, it will work.

I like direct advertising, but I'm not foolish enough to say it's the only kind you should use. People who sell products for general usage are better off blanketing the community, for example. Advertising—in whatever form you choose—should be custom-made for your personality, your product, your demographics, and your place in the market.

Ego—Again

I've talked about ego earlier in the book, but it should be mentioned again in the context of advertising. One of the ugliest men I have known insisted on having his picture adorn all his company's billboards. Perhaps people like to do business with ugly people, but I suspect it didn't accomplish anything except to stroke his ego.

These days, there's a big drive for chief executives to become company spokesmen. Lee Iacocca did it with extraordinary success, building the bandwagon for everyone else to jump on. He is a dynamic and personable spokesman, with a great P.R. campaign. But some of the automatons getting on television these days are doing their products no good.

If you are paying for an ad campaign, there is a temptation to become famous at the same time. Why not? Because it may hurt your product. Ask yourself how much of it is ego gratification and how much is meant to attract new business.

Admarketingsales

It's hard to separate advertising, marketing, and selling. They are all vital functions that overlap to form one package, and they all have to fit together for the whole to work. No business can be concerned just with marketing, to the detriment of advertising or vice versa. Sales, marketing, and advertising managers have to work together as a coordinated team.

To prevent confusion, a company should project a cohesive image. To do this, all divisions have to tell the same story. The organization of this effort depends on the size of the company, of course. If it is a one-man shop, then the man who puts the marketing program together also produces the brochure and other advertising materials—perhaps even trains his sales force. If it is a large company with segmented departments, the key to a cohesive image is to ensure continuous coordination.

The ultimate goal is to reach the customer and close the sale. A well-directed, intelligent, and measurable advertising campaign will make your product known and get people to buy it.

13

Creating an Organization

When I had been in business only for a few months as Jack Nadel, Inc., I began to train new salesmen. My father-in-law, who had invested in the business, stopped in at the office one day and saw me talking to the men.

He was concerned at what he saw as a waste of my abilities. He took me to one side and said, "Son, I don't know what you're doing. You can sell so much more than anyone else here; why are you bothering to train them? Why don't you just go out and sell?"

It was true, I admitted, I could sell more than anyone else. "But if I do it all myself," I explained, "then ten years from now I'll still be trying to do it all myself. I've got to train people who can create the business."

It happens to every entrepreneur. As soon as you start to succeed, you reach the point where you have to count on someone else. You know in your heart that the person will never do it as well as you've done it, or your customers are used to having it done, but sooner or later you have to trust someone else.

The greatest ideas in the world have come to nothing because of a lack of organization. And countless businesses have failed for the same reason. No man is an island, and no man can do it all himself, no matter how much he'd like to. Perhaps it was possible once, but it's not possible in 1987. Everything has become unbelievably complicated. There is no such thing as a simple business anymore.

I used to hear successful business people boast about their ulcers, saying, "I'm the first one in in the morning and the last one there at night," as if testifying to their courage and hard work. Well, the reality is that the world doesn't pay for hard work; it pays for results—on what you accomplish. On the other hand, people constantly ask me how I run all these companies and people, and how I'm able to accomplish all the things I do without being a slave to the company. It's because I have an organization.

Good organization is absolutely essential for the smallest business as well as the largest corporations. It's bad organization that causes the military to pay such outrageous prices for stock merchandise. In most cases it's not dishonesty; it is a lack of training and motivation on the part of the people doing the buying. This seems more common in large organizations, and it appears that the larger an organization gets, the less efficient it becomes. There are enough exceptions, however, to support my contention that this is not a given, but occurs simply because an organization hasn't been properly set up in the first place. If the roots are weak, the tree just gets shakier and shakier as it grows taller.

The real purpose of an organizational structure is to build a permanent company. The stronger your organization, the easier it is for your company to grow and prosper. A strong organization takes two basic ingredients: a realistic look at the philosophy and purpose of the company and the creation of policies to attain that purpose; and the people you hire to carry out that purpose.

The people you hire are more important than anything else. You can draw up many sophisticated flowcharts, organization tables, graphs, and titles, but without people, you simply don't have an organization. And without good people, you don't have a good organization. Success depends upon the quality of the people you hire.

The building of an organization is an enormous subject, and I'm not wise or arrogant enough to tell everyone how to organize a business. What I can do, however, is relate my methodology—what has worked for me over years of trial and error—in the hope you will glean some insights.

Managing People

Unfortunately, organizations do not suddenly materialize. Creating an organization takes a great deal of time and hardship. At the outset I had to put in many 7-day weeks and 15-hour days; and I made my share of mistakes. But if done properly, with the correct premises, an organization makes life a hell of a lot easier.

The first thing I had to do was train salespeople because that's what my company did—sell. I had to find people I thought were right, and I had to train them in my style so that they reflected my business philosophy. Then I had to make sure they made more money with me than they could with anyone else, in order to keep them.

One of the reasons I went into business for myself was because I disagreed with a basic policy of the company I worked for. They hired their sales force on a commission basis as independent contractors. I wanted something more permanent, so I had to see what kind of policy I could set to attract great people, keep them, and increase my sales. I made three rules to accomplish this:

1. The salesperson had to work exclusively for Jack Nadel, Inc. In an industry where salesmen carried three different order books, this was unusual. But I insisted that there be no side deals or contracts whatsoever.
2. Salespeople had to become employees. This was expensive because I had to pay withholding taxes and

benefits, but it gave me and them a situation with some permanence.
3. The salesperson had to be someone I could be really proud of.

At that time I wanted no one who came from the specialty advertising industry because, to my mind, they were all badly trained. If I were training someone to swing a golf club, I'd find it a lot easier to train someone who had never swung one before than someone who had acquired a lot of bad habits. Business was no different.

The program was to hire one person at a time, who agreed to work exclusively for me. Then I would train him. At that time, the simplest way I knew to train someone was to take him out and make calls. To this day, I guess I'm short on theory and long on action.

Our procedures are much more sophisticated today, but they rest on the same basics. You hire the individual you think best and go out with him to see how he acts. The first day I would explain the business, the second and third days I would make all the sales presentations, then, on the fourth day, I would give him the sample and say, "You're on. You make the call." After that, I would leave him to flounder for two weeks, then go back with him to see what he had learned. The methodology may have been primitive by today's standards, but it worked.

It took time and effort to train salespeople because I didn't have a big budget, but it was the best and most inexpensive way at the time to build an organization. It couldn't have been too bad. In my first year of business, I hired three people. One worked for me for 12 years, another worked with me until he retired in 1984, and the third, Sherman Teller, today is a senior vice president, marking his 34th year.

Managing people is a skill. Some people find it difficult and try to ignore it, but a businessman running a company can't afford to do that for long. I don't know if there's such a thing as a born leader; I think it takes a lot of work, plus trial and error.

Accountability

Over the years, one of the lessons I learned was that to manage people well, you have to make them all responsible for something and give them no place to hide. Many companies are destroyed because they don't give their people authority, and they give them too many places to hide. In the act of making a decision, you expose yourself. An organization can be struck with paralysis when employees are unwilling to make decisions and thus expose themselves.

In our company, executives are always accountable, with an assigned responsibility for a certain segment of the business. They know it, and consequently they perform better. They also appreciate having the responsibilities known; there are no mysteries. Furthermore, if you give someone the responsibility to make decisions, never second-guess his judgment calls. When an executive is berated constantly for calling the wrong shots, he is no longer willing to act. Instead he always looks over his shoulder for your approval.

Another common failing is giving people responsibility without giving them the authority to carry through on it. You can't do that. I learned in the Air Force that there were only three answers to any questions an officer put to you: "Yes, Sir. No, Sir. No Excuse, Sir." It's true. There are no acceptable excuses, except to say, "I screwed up." Then you say, "Okay, don't do it again." And the discussion ends.

People with responsibility and no authority cannot fairly be held accountable, and that's a bad situation. I've been given the excuse that something wasn't done because, "the person who works under me is inefficient." My answer to that is, "No excuse. You're saying you're inefficient. I didn't hire the person who works below you, and it's not my job to fire him.

That's your job, so do it." Of course, if you give people authority, they have to be willing to exercise it, or all the effort is wasted.

Measuring Productivity

To manage its people successfully, a company must have measuring sticks and checkpoints. You can't judge people on the brightness of their smiles or their apparent willingness to perform. Too many arbitrary and unfair viewpoints can enter into the picture. You have to judge people on their productivity.

Productivity is easy to do in sales. Either a person has made his quota or hasn't. There's no place to hide. But productivity is more difficult to judge in financial and administrative positions. It is difficult, but never impossible. For example, you can set up a measuring stick that says the person in charge of accounts receivable has to keep them within 60 days. Going higher up the ladder, you can set parameters of money management for your chief financial officer. What cost-cutting measures can he come up with, or how viable is the financial health of the company? The person in charge of production has to see that production happens as scheduled, that deliveries are made on time, and that internal accidents are kept to a minimum. You can do it for every position in a company by pinpointing the activity of the individual.

When the matter is not that simple, do it with cross-checks. In our direct mail company, for instance, the computer department is constantly checked on projects by running an internal cost-control analysis on the work done, then having that work quoted on the outside. If it's cheaper to do it on the outside, we have either to look at our procedures or consider the wisdom of keeping all that equipment and personnel.

In our manufacturing facilities, all machines have a quota. But to carry it even further, we separate each department in our manufacturing facilities and make each a profit center. They are all directly measurable and all accountable.

People are also paid on this basis. And, most important, they all know they have to deal with two elements. On one hand, if they don't deliver, they can always be demoted or lose their jobs. But on the other (which we like to talk about more), they know that *compensation* is geared to productivity. If they achieve certain goals, they get increases. Employees have to feel that, by performing better, they not only advance the cause of the company but also their own causes. Many people will vow love and affection for the company, but if we don't pay them well or if we fall through on our side of the deal, we lose them.

In every job—be it sales, industrial safety, financing, security, administration, or whatever—there have to be objective measuring sticks, and individuals have to feel they directly benefit by doing a better job.

Wherever possible, promote from within. If someone does a particularly good job, he or she is not only properly compensated for it, but has a chance to advance. Those people who have more dedication, spirit, and thoughtfulness in the job should be rewarded. It's not only good for them, but it's the only way a company can get better.

I feel an employee almost never leaves a company, but that a company leaves the employee. But you walk a fine line trying to understand the needs of employees without acting like a big brother. It is impossible to accommodate all needs, and you can't get involved in the personal affairs of employees, lest it become an endless diversion from your central goals.

I once had an employee whom I really liked. She seemed to be intelligent, to have all the needed capabilities, and showed a tremendous love for the company. But she just didn't perform. I tried to accommodate her, but she destroyed whatever department she was in. Finally, I had to say good-bye, even though it was very difficult.

Being Tough

Probably the toughest thing I ever have to do is fire somebody. But if you're running a business, the desire to be loved can't dominate your thinking. You also have to be able to do what has to be done, and this applies particularly to terminating employees.

Most of the time, when you have to fire someone, you are not only doing yourself but your employee a favor. If he or she is a fish out of water, there is a different pond to swim in. It doesn't do a business any good to carry deadweight or negative people. The old saying that a rotten apple can spoil the whole barrel applies here, too. A negative influence in any department can destroy the department and eventually the company.

Toughness is a necessary quality, but it also has to be temperate and fair. If you set guidelines for a company, you have to execute those guidelines. If someone fails to stick to them, he or she has to be either corrected or terminated.

Our contract with our salespeople stipulates they have no outside deals. On one occasion I caught one of our top salesmen with an outside deal and hauled him over the coals. He swore he would never do it again. The second time I caught him I let him go. If I hadn't, it would have jarred everything. Our other employees would have thought the rules were worthless, that they had no teeth.

On another occasion, I had an executive headquartered in New York who turned in outrageous expense accounts. I met with my financial man at the time, and he proposed a string of safeguards to prevent this individual from spending us into oblivion for his own purposes. I went along with it and listened and then, finally, something just stuck in my gut. "I've spoken to him about this half a dozen times and nothing seems to have any effect," I said. "I will not act as a policeman. I'm going to let him go."

My financial man was shocked. "But who will replace him?" he asked.

"I don't know," I said. "But I can't continue to be a policeman. And I can't keep allowing this to happen. We're letting him go." And that's what we did. It helped form one of my major rules: I never try to police my staff. If I have to act as a policeman at my salary, there is something very wrong.

A great deal of a company's success depends upon the integrity it has to its own goals. And these goals have to be zealously guarded with toughness, temperance, and fairness.

Fairness involves judgment. If an individual has been with you for ten years, has done a terrific job, and then makes a mistake, don't summarily fire him. Anyone can have a temporary aberration, and you don't destroy him for that. It is a question of degree. Any strong company can take a certain amount of damage or incompetence, but there is a point at which it begins to do irreparable harm. It is always best to act immediately when that happens or, preferably, just before it happens.

You have to compromise all through your business life, but at a certain point you draw the line. Remember as a kid when you drew a line in the dirt and said, "Pass that line and you're dead"? When your friend stepped across the line, you drew another a little farther back and said, "Alright. Pass *this* line and you're dead." Well, you can't do that when you're running a company. The location of the line has to be known and understood. When someone crosses it, he has to know that the consequences will be applied. You can't be so hard-nosed you never bend, but you must be tough enough to act decisively when you have to.

Organizational Structure

In setting up our parent company, Measured Marketing Services, we began with an examination of the philosophy. Who are we? What are we trying to do? Who are we trying to serve? How can we best accomplish our goals? Any organization has to start with those questions.

Our first decision was to make the corporate headquarters very small. The headquarters doesn't produce anything. It doesn't make sales or create income. Therefore, it doesn't justify a gigantic overhead.

The second decision was that each division be autonomous. A lot of companies pay lip service to the autonomy of divisions, but in reality the head office is on their backs all the time. In our structure, each division is a separate company, with it's own president or chief executive officer, it's own chief operations officer, and it's own chief financial officer and financial staff. Each runs itself. The corporate office doesn't get involved in the day-to-day affairs of each business.

Because corporate headquarters is not involved in the daily grind, it can perform its primary functions. These are to be removed from the divisions enough to see where the trouble spots are, to ensure that the company stays on the charted course, and to create the future of the company. Headquarters can't be so inundated with daily activity and fire-watching that it doesn't see the forest for the trees, and is thus blind to the opportunities out there.

Corporate headquarters gets a constant flow of information from the divisions so that it can see what new businesses to go into and can guide the financial destiny of the company. It keeps track of the receivables, payables, inventory levels, and so on of each division through simplified monthly reports which tell what business has been done that month. When a danger signal pops up, headquarters checks into it.

Simplicity is one of the criteria. When complexity enters any procedure, it creates rather than solves problems. Each division's primary function is to make profits. We keep inspection of that as simple as possible. And we don't step in unless the division isn't performing that function.

When you allow a company true autonomy, you have to be very careful with the personnel you choose. The trust factor is enormous. You have given them responsibility; now you must be willing to give them the authority to carry it through.

In each of our divisions, the top executives are a mix of homegrown people trained in our methodology and way of doing business and people who have come from outside. We have found this to be a workable formula, and we try to stick to it.

In Jack Nadel, Inc., for example, Marty Nadel is president and C.E.O.; Sherman Teller, who joined the company in 1953, is senior vice president. Both are homegrown. Marty is a great salesman and head of the company, while Sherman, who knows where the ship has been, helps guide where it is going by providing steady counsel. But then we needed someone who comes from outside with an entirely different viewpoint, someone who can bring something new to the company. In that respect, we have Russ Woodlief as executive vice president. He came from a major competitor and brought with him a number of salespeople and an amazing ability to build and maintain a sales force.

We can never be so egotistical as to think that we know it all or that everything good comes from us. When someone joins from outside the company, there is a blending of workable ideas and a discarding of unworkable concepts. It's the way an alloy is stronger than pure metal.

The same situation exists at Krupp-Taylor. It is headed by my partner Bob Buckingham, a man who probably knows more about direct mail than anyone else in the world. His right hand is Norton Weinstein who, in addition to being an account supervisor, knows more about the inside of a plant than anyone else. He has a rare combination of sales, administrative, and manufacturing knowhow. When the company was reorganized, he became the executive vice president of operations.

Our manufacturing company, Art-Mold/Pierre Cardin, has another of my partners, Harold Holland, as chief executive officer, with Mel Hyman, who was also raised in the business and has been with the company for 26 years, as executive vice president.

These are three different companies. Krupp-Taylor does direct mail; Jack Nadel, Inc., is a distributor, and Art-Mold/Pierre Cardin is a manufacturer. But the theory holds in all of them. In each, three skills have been brought together to make a dynamic and unique organization. When you put skilled, creative, and motivated people together, not only are they going to fulfill their primary function, but they will create something you can't even predict. And this is what has made Measured Marketing Services explode.

Corporate headquarters is set up in essentially the same way. I didn't need sales or creative people, but I needed the best financial officer I could find, because that was one of our main functions. In this case I brought in from the outside Hugh Pierce as my chief financial officer. He had a background with major accounting firms such as Arthur Andersen and field experience with an operating company. The chief financial officer in each division reports to him. My other strong right arm is Beverly Cohn, who runs internal communications and operates as director of research and development. All communications funnel through her, plus, if I have a special project, she follows through on it. Together, these two people perform functions that leave me free enough as chief executive officer to act as a catalyst in the company and provide leadership.

This is not a complex system of organization. I doubt the theory behind it would fill a college textbook, but it is a workable system that has enabled our company to grow almost tenfold in as many years. If it wasn't a good organization, I would not have been able to create as many ideas or accomplish as much as I have. But like any good organization, it began with the philosophy and evolved over time into the living organism it is. There is a workable structure, but it is not so stratified as to be unwieldy or to resist change when it is necessary.

Business today, particularly when involved in international trade, has to be able to act quickly, to change direction on a dime, and to respond rapidly to market needs. To do this without severe disruption demands excellent organization. It is not something that can be created overnight, but it is something to constantly strive for.

14

Completing the Circle

It was 5:00 A.M. on New Year's Day, 1946. It had been a hell
of a party.

It was also the end of an era. The terror, excitement, and
glamour of three and a half years in the Air Force was over.
There would be no more endless hours navigating a wounded
plane back to its home base. I would no longer suffer the
bone-crushing weariness that came with 15-hour missions. And
the rewards were over, too: coming home a hero to open arms
and no price tag, to the amazing gratitude of citizens, and to
the beautiful women who flocked to the uniform. It was all
about to end.

I took off my uniform for the last time. I began with the
cap with the Fifty Mission Crush, then the jacket with the
Silver Bars on the shoulders, the Air Force Wings on the
chest, the battle ribbons, the medals, the Distinguished Flying
Cross, the Air Medal with Four Oak Leaf Clusters, and the
Presidential Citation. After hanging up the uniform, I polished
each medal and placed it in the appropriate velvet-lined box.

I had turned down an offer to re-enlist. I was ready to
strike out on my own, to act as an individual, rather than as
part of a unit. I was young and cocky, and it was time to
start my career as a civilian.

On January 2, 1946, dressed in a glen-plaid suit I wouldn't be caught dead in today, I marched to the unemployment office to register and make myself available for a job interview. It was my first encounter with an ungrateful civilian. When I told him I was a salesman, he asked what kind of experience I'd had. "I was a navigator-bombardier. I flew twenty-seven combat missions," I said.

He looked at me with a tired expression. "There really is no market out there for someone with those particular skills, and I don't see how that helps you as a salesman."

Before the Army, I had been a delivery boy, a truck driver's helper, and a shipfitter's apprentice. But in my Air Force years I had attained a certain amount of confidence and learned to mix with people. If I wanted something, I usually found a way to get it. I also felt that, after surviving the war, I could succeed at anything. I knew that if I went into sales I would be successful. I felt in my bones that this would be my skill.

I turned to the employment counsellor and said, "Look, just put 'sales' down as my occupation. That's what it's going to be from now on. If you have a place for me to go, I'll get the job." I was the sixth veteran interviewed for the position of apprentice salesman at Stevens & Thompson Paper Mills. After two interviews, I was hired.

As I had known I would be, I was a good salesman and soon became one of the best in the company. Partly as a result of my efforts, they went from an unprofitable operation to having a huge backlog.

After I had been there for about six months, one of the paper distributors to whom I sold offered me a job as a commission salesman. With them I sold a whole range of paper products, and again I did well.

I was on the brink of success in the paper business, but a vision kept intruding. I had spent one weekend in Los Angeles before going overseas in 1944, and I had loved it. At the time, I promised myself that if I survived the war, I would live there. I knew that if I didn't make the move now, I never would.

My older brother, Saul, was already living there, so I decided to join him. I gave up my job, bought a 1940 Hudson automobile, and put an ad in the newspaper for someone to share expenses for a cross-country trip. Two men answered.

In a car that could barely do 55 M.P.H., we drove from New York to Los Angeles in two and a half days. Los Angeles was as I remembered it. The weather was gorgeous, the streets were wide, and everything seemed fresh and new. I dropped off my passengers and drove to my brother's apartment.

When I arrived, I realized that one of the riders had taken my baggage. All I had was literally the shirt on my back and the $30 in my pocket. So began my big adventure in my new hometown—Los Angeles.

My business odyssey has taken more than 40 years. Like any journey, it has had its hardships and losses, but these have been far outweighed by the satisfactions of accomplishment and the rewards that go with it.

A Personal View of Business

While in the process of living my life—doing the business; making the deals; creating the products; hiring the people; doing the buying, selling, advertising, and organizing—I have not been totally aware of the effects it all has had on my thinking. I do know that, although people talk about almost everything in the business world in terms of personal gain, it may begin there but it does not end there. The edges of business and personal life overlap so much that I am hard-pressed to say where one begins and the other ends. The fact is, business has always been a pleasure.

For example, I have a close and intimate relationship with each of my three partners. I couldn't say whether I think of them more as business associates or as personal friends. I also bring my business home at night, not as a hardship or a weight on my wife, Elly, but as a point of common interest. She helped me start the business and is still totally aware of almost everything I do. She also adds a special dimension by listening and making informed suggestions. We are both aware that the business is a personal, living entity.

Business overlaps into other areas as well. During my early business years there was a great hullabaloo in the United States over the McCarthy hearings on unAmerican activities. Since we lived in Los Angeles and had many friends in Hollywood, we were very aware of the fear that dominated the times. For every courageous individual who spoke up to express his true feelings, there were a hundred who hid behind whatever barricades they could put up.

I'm a card-carrying capitalist, but as a voracious reader and student of history, I am interested in politics and social movements. I remember one day taking my copy of Karl Marx's *Das Kapital* off the shelf, fearsome that someone would see it and think I had "Communistic tendencies." I was ashamed of that, and put the book back on the shelf. Since then, Elly and I have never felt it necessary to hide our beliefs. Over the years, we have been involved in many political and charitable causes. In the first sales lecture I ever attended, it was stated never to talk about religion, sex, or politics. But these topics are a great deal of what everyone is all about, and sometimes they cannot be ignored.

During the Vietnam War, I was one of the original group of business people who felt the war was not something we should be involved in. Some of my associates at the time were horrified that I would not only take such a position, but give speeches about it. Of course, over 58,000 Americans were sacrificed in that far-off country. Aside from the inhumanity and horror of that loss, the war was the worst thing for the world of business. War may be good for the defense establishment and their suppliers, but ultimately it is bad for business. If the ultimate war ever occurs, there will be no business.

The business community is as divided in its beliefs as is any other group. But I have always felt that it is the responsibility of each element to make itself heard. Business has other responsibilities, too. On one hand, it creates employment, new products, and luxuries and it raises our standard of living and quality of life. On the other, it has been responsible for intimidation, injustice, greed, short-sightedness, and all the other accusations that have been leveled. All of them are true, and all are false. Nothing is cut-and-dried.

Today, business has its best face forward. Unlike the traumatic sixties and seventies, when young people sneered at the successes of their parents, today's youngsters come out of school wanting to emulate those successes and extend them to new frontiers. To a great degree, it is to this audience I present the methodology, feelings, and philosophy that comes from my experience in the business world.

It has been pronounced that to succeed in business you have to leave in your wake the corpses of people you have stepped on. Television prime-time soaps portray businessmen as ruthless and unethical. Books have been written on how to intimidate your opponents. This isn't my world. I have always looked at business as an area in which individuals can creatively express themselves—without the killer instinct. Professional boxers need the killer instinct; professional businessmen do not. The goal is not to put people away or put other businesses down, but to build your business up.

I have little patience with the "dynamic," single-minded hard-driving businessman. I think he does society little service. I would like to see business schools give courses in the humanities, and I would like to see the liberal arts schools give courses in business. When people are wellrounded, they become better citizens and serve themselves, their families, and their communities more fully because they have an understanding of the other end of the spectrum. The artist would undoubtedly be better off with some basic business training that could enable him to deal and sell the most important commodity he has—himself and his talent. And, by the same token, the stereotypical businessman with an ulcer would be better off tempering his hard drive with the soft sounds of the arts.

Business is itself part science, part art. Like life, it is a complex affair. If I were to sum up the advice I give, it is, first, to always be a professional. Whatever it is you choose to do, know your position and do it well. Second, be flexible. Business conditions change and the world changes with them. It's great to read about how the captain goes down with the sinking ship, but that really doesn't serve anyone's purpose. The ability to change direction—not frivolously but when really necessary—often spells the difference between success and failure. Third, when you attain some success, pay attention to the world around you. Nothing productive has ever come from being a hermit, and no man really lives by himself. We live together in this world, and it is the business person's responsibility to make the world a little better.

Business and Society

Competition is one of the healthiest facets of our society. It forces you to do better and brings out the best in everyone. Taken in its broadest context, competition and free enterprise have built in the United States the greatest economy ever known. It would be the worst crime to let it deteriorate.

Recently, I heard an incredible statement. There was a discussion of S.D.I.—the "Star Wars" proposal—and one of the proponents of the program said that he realized it was enormously expensive and that it was going to drain our economy, but he was for it. The Soviets would have to match our program, and we could afford the drain better than they could.

An entire school of political philosophy has arisen based on the concept that we should fight an economic war of attrition with the Soviets. We should not concentrate on elevating the standards of people all over the world, but instead bring everything down so that in the end we will have more resources than the Soviets, who will collapse economically against this suffocating military burden. It is an unbelievable concept, and it is deadly—for both the Soviet Union and the United States.

There must be a better solution. If, for instance, a disarmament proposal could be achieved, the world would see prosperity it never dreamed of. Instead, we spend an incomprehensible amount of money for destructive weapons that don't feed anyone, that don't provide shelter for anyone—in short, that accomplish little except the dubious achievement of obsoleting themselves every few years so they then have to be replaced.

We face an economic crisis in which the imbalance in international trade plays a large part. Unfortunately, the mammoth U.S. military budget is diverting our technology into military and related establishments, thus depriving the private sector of the creativity and capability it needs to face the challenges of this crisis. Contrast our situation with that of Japan, which has virtually no defense budget. Note where all the consumer products are coming from today. The Japanese industrialists think we are crazy, and rightly so.

Our brightest minds are busy creating the greatest defense establishment in the history of the world—one that could collapse economically.

There are no simple solutions to the problems we are facing. Even the relationship between the communist and capitalist worlds has grown increasingly complex since World War II. The Soviets and China haven't agreed on anything in years, and there is dissension among the United States and its allies. There isn't much a single businessman can do to move against these giant world currents except assert himself whenever possible and speak up when he should.

I have cautioned you not to go against the grain and to move with the tide, but there are also responsibilities involved in being a part of society. Certain issues are worth fighting about. There are times when principle should prevail—not by tilting at windmills or going down with the ship, but by working within the bounds of reality. These are personal decisions we all have to make. Business *can* be ethical, it *can* be rational, it *can* be concerned with the greater good of the community and of country and mankind. If future generations recognize and strive for these ideals, it will be.

A Backward Glance

As I look back on my business life, there are moments that stick in my mind. Some are watershed moments; others are personal and inexplicable. All are important to me. These are some of the highlights that come to mind:

When we made the deal to have Jack Nadel, Inc., acquired by Republic Corporation, there was a tax-free exchange of stock. This was complicated, however, by the fact that my brother Marty and I owned the building in which Jack Nadel, Inc., was housed. Republic asserted that the real estate would constitute a conflict of interest and that we should sell it to them along with the business. We had no problem with that, but we insisted that they pay cash for the real estate. The building was appraised and valued at $200,000. Republic agreed to our terms.

The day came to close the deal, and the executive negotiating for Republic took me aside, saying "Everything is fine, all the papers are in order, but we decided to give you stock for the real estate," he said.

"That wasn't the deal," I said, surprised.

"Well, that's the deal we have to make. We are not going to pay cash for it," he said.

"Then don't buy the real estate—just lease it from me," I suggested.

He shook his head. "We can't do that. It's a conflict of interest."

"Let me make myself clear," I said. "I'm not selling the real estate for stock. You either pay cash for it or lease it."

"Do you mean to say that you'd blow the deal right now for that?" he asked incredulously, but a threat was implied in his question.

I learned early in business that you can't allow yourself to be intimidated. If someone hits you with a strong statement, come back with a stronger one. I could have hedged and suggested that maybe we could discuss it, but I didn't. Instead I said: "Not only would I blow the deal right now, but in exactly two minutes I'm walking out of here and there is no deal. That's the deal we made, and that's the deal that stands, or there is no deal." I kept the property and leased it to Republic. We still own it to this day and recently refinanced it for $1.2 million.

My move into the world of a New York conglomerate was a major turning point in my career. I could have continued my business career buying and selling advertising specialty merchandise. Instead I entered an entirely new world run by business-school people who dealt in theory and projections and who juggled numbers like balls.

I learned much in those years. I saw the absolute impossibility of any management running 90 disparate companies with any degree of success. I saw the tremendous waste of time and money put into pet projects. I saw avarice and stupidity. But I also learned many disciplines that I never before knew existed. I had run my business by the seat of my pants, but I learned the necessity to project sales, profits, expenses, and cash flow. I learned about bank lines, facilities, and people. It was a tremendous experience. Republic Corporation was my college course in corporate business. I learned the rules and regulations. Some I kept and some I discarded, but all in all, I was the better for it.

I had only read about the French Riviera and seen it in the movies. Then I visited Cannes, in the south of France, for the first time. We sat at a sidewalk café on the *croisette* (beachfront). The people around us wore exotic costumes and were different from any I had seen before. Languages swirled around me: French, German, Spanish, Italian, Danish, even English. It was tremendously exciting; I was doing business, and it was truly international. As I talked to these people from different cultures, I realized again what a wonderfully interesting world we live in, and how revitalizing a tonic it was to drink from.

In 1956, I visited a factory in Tokyo. Only ten years earlier, I had bombed the same area. It was a casting factory where they manufactured antimony, which is molten lead, for desk lighters.

It was all a hand operation. I watched them stick the die into the fire, pour molten lead into the receptacle, pour it out by hand, and then bang out the excess flash. The equipment and the process were unbelievably primitive. I turned to my American agent and asked, "How could these people have possibly started a war with this kind of technology?"

Thirty years later, I look at modern-day Japan and realize the incredible progress they have made. But it hasn't been without cost. I had the privilege of walking the streets of Japan when half the people wore kimonos. Now there are modern hotels, sophisticated equipment, and the highest degree of technology available. You never see a kimono. Japanese businessmen are very intense and look more harried than their American counterparts. There has been a loss of grace.

In 1978, I remember the excitement of giving a talk at an international show in Düsseldorf, before an audience of 2,000 disbelieving people. A huge cloud of smoke hovered in the room (everyone in West Germany smokes) and over my head was a gigantic screen, translating my English remarks into German, because more than 50 percent of the people didn't speak English.

It was a very American speech—open and optimistic (qualities not native to European business). I knew I hit a chord, however, when I was complimented afterwards in ten different languages. People really appreciated what I had to say, and it was the first time I felt I had something of worth to pass on to my fellows.

Just two years ago in Tokyo, Albert Lucky and I were walking the eight blocks from a factory back to our hotel because we had been unable to find a taxi. We each lugged a heavy bag of merchandise through the narrow, busy streets. Suddenly, I put my bag down in the middle of the street and looked around me. I turned to Albert and said incredulously, "What the hell am I doing? I'm a damn multimillionaire. What am I doing here?"

And he laughed and said, "It keeps you young."

My older brother, Saul, had a real impact on my life. He embodied the entrepreneurial spirit. Over the years he had four wives and lost three fortunes. He was a brawler, a gambler, and an alcoholic; he thought nothing of going to Las Vegas and blowing $50,000 or $100,000. Somehow, he was always able to make a comeback.

Saul was an absolutely brilliant salesman, with a powerful personality that was totally persuasive. He could put impossible deals together, and I learned a lot from him. But he was a trader rather than a long-range business operator. Because Saul was tough—if not impossible—to work for, he could never build an organization. I learned a great deal from that as well, particularly how you can only build with good people who are allowed to express themselves and to grow.

Above all, I remember people. I remember when the factory in France was at a particularly low ebb, having great difficulty. There is a distributor in Brussels, Jacques von Bravel, who had become a friend and one of my major fans because of a speech I had given.

I called him and said, "Jacques, I really need your help. Could you fly down to Cannes to be with me for a couple of days?"

"But of course," he said, without a moment's hesitation.

The next day I got a telex from him saying that all flights were booked. "Instead of calling you, I just left in my automobile," it read.

He drove from Brussels, Belgium, to the south of France strictly because of loyalty and friendship. It was a remarkable,

remarkable thing to me. It is one of many fine relationships that I now enjoy.

Today, after more than 40 years in business, I am considered successful. Most important, I have a very good feeling within myself. Whatever success I have attained, it has not been at the expense of anyone else. The people I have met have had dramatic impacts on my life, but I know that I, too, have affected their lives. Were I not here, their lives would be different. I couldn't ask for or expect much more than that.

I have tried to show that business is a great adventure—as great as exploring uncharted seas or climbing unconquered mountains. It is an adventure of personal expansion which, if conducted honorably, can only enhance you and the people you come into contact with.

Now more than ever business in the United States must expand both geographically and conceptually to meet the economic challenges of the present and future. It is not something that will be done by governments. It will take individuals who are willing to do what must be done.

Expansion can be a harrowing, frightening experience, particularly if you are an individual dealing with your own resources. But little of value is attained without some risk. You have a choice. Either you fear the unknown or, like visionary explorers of the past, you can face it as a challenge to overcome, a battle to win. The journey will leave you all the better for it. When I turned 60, I sent this piece of philosophy as part of the invitation to celebrate the occasion:

The Secret of Survival

The Secret of Survival, when I was a boy on the streets of New York, was to hit hard, move fast, and have friends I could count on.

The Secret of Survival, when I flew in combat as a young man, was to hit hard, move fast, and have friends I could count on.

The Secret of Survival, when I started in business, was
to hit hard, move fast, and have friends I could count on.

The Secret of Survival, as I now approach 60, is understanding that the need to hit hard and move fast is greatly
diminished. But the importance of friends and the capacity
for friendship grows stronger with each passing year.

The patterns in our lives are wonderful and strange.
Nothing brought this home to me more profoundly than an
incident a couple of years ago when Elly and I were overseas.
It was 1985, and my wife and I were sitting in a small bar,
enjoying an intimate cocktail with Jungi Hiromori. Jungi ran
the family business, started by his father 35 years earlier; he
had just become our exclusive licensee and distributor in Japan.

It was 4:00 P.M., and the bar was unusually quiet and
empty. I was very impressed by Jungi. He had been an intelligent and gracious host in Tokyo, and both Elly and I felt
a close friendship building. As we lifted our glasses in a toast,
I asked Jungi about his history. He told us about the business
and how he had taken control when his father died six years
earlier. "Were you born in Tokyo?" I asked.

"Yes," he said. "I was born in 1942 in Tokyo, but I left
when the children were evacuated to the small towns during
the air raids."

I felt a sudden chill. "Do you remember the air raids?"
I asked.

"Not really," he replied. "But I was told of the great
B-29s that rained death on the city."

There was a pause, and then he said, "Although I can't
remember the actual raids, the memory must be inside me.
For many years, when I heard an airplane, I would shudder
in fear and cry out."

I pictured once again flying over Tokyo, crying "Bombs
Away" as I gave the order to release the explosives on the
crowded city below. Only now I could also see the incompre-
hension of a terror-stricken little boy of three, crying out at
the death and destruction that came from the sky.

I wanted to reach out and embrace Jungi, to tell him of the sadness I felt. Instead, I stared at him for a moment and said, "How terrible it had to be for you."

In a single moment, past and future met. Much had happened to the brash young war hero to make him the mature businessman who now sat opposite Jungi. After those exciting yet destructive early years, there had been half a lifetime of satisfaction and achievement in his chosen arena. He was still the same man, but infinitely more experienced and hopefully wiser. It was as if after 40 years a circle had been completed.

Index